Living on the Bott

Frontispiece 1. A view of the Boott Cotton Millyard published in Gleason's Pictorial *in 1852*

Frontispiece 2. Boston University graduate students excavating a well discovered in the rear yard of Boott Boardinghouse Unit #48

Living on the Boott

Historical Archaeology at the Boott Mills
Boardinghouses, Lowell, Massachusetts

Stephen A. Mrozowski,
Grace H. Ziesing, and Mary C. Beaudry

University of Massachusetts Press
Amherst

Copyright ©1996 by the Lowell Historic Preservation Commission
All rights reserved
Printed in the United States of America
LC 95-52177
ISBN 1-55849-034-5 (cloth); 035-3 (pbk.)
Designed by Sally Nichols
Set in New Baskerville
Printed and bound by Thomson-Shore, Inc.

Library of Congress Cataloging-in-Publication data

Mrozowski, Stephen A.
    Living on the Boott : historical archaeology at the Boott Mills Boardinghouses,
Lowell, Massachusetts / Stephen A. Mrozowski, Grace H. Ziesing, and Mary C.
Beaudry.
                    p.   cm.
    Includes bibliographical references and index.
    ISBN 1-55849-034-5 (cloth : alk. paper). — ISBN 1-55849-035-3
(pbk. : alk. paper)
    1. Lowell (Mass.)—Antiquities. 2. Archaeology and history—Massachusetts—
Lowell. 3. Boot Mills (Lowell, Mass.) 4. Boardinghouses—Massachusetts—Lowell.
5. Working class—Massachusetts—Lowell—History.
I. Ziesing, Grace H. II. Beaudry, Mary Carolyn, 1950–   . III. Title.
F74.L9M76   1996
974.4'4—dc20   95-52177
                                                                CIP

British Library Cataloguing in Publication data are available.

This book is published with the support and cooperation of the University of
Massachusetts Boston and the Lowell Historic Preservation Commission.

Both of us would like to thank Grace Ziesing for her kindness in allowing us to dedicate this book to the memories of our fathers,

Eugene James Beaudry and
Stephen Albert Mrozowski Sr.

Contents

List of Illustrations   ix

Preface   xi

Introduction   1

    The Boott Mills and Its Boardinghouses   4

    Archaeology in a Parking Lot   9

Historical Archaeology in Context   13

    Tools of the Trade   15

    Putting the Pieccs Together   34

    Archaeology at the Boott Mills   36

Lowell's Urban Landscape   38

    A Landscape Changed   38

The Planned City   39
The Backyard Story   43

Living Conditions of Boott Mills Workers   49

Life in an Urban Boardinghouse   50
Sanitation   52
Hygiene   53
Health   55
The Personal Touch   57

Mealtimes at the Boott   59

Working-Class Meals   60
A Telling Comparison   64

Leisure Time at the Boott   66

Cigars and Cutties   67
Alcohol   71
Postscript   74

Clothing and Personal Adornment   75

Jewelry and Beads   77
Hair Combs and Ornaments   78
Buttons and Studs   79

The Bigger Picture   81

Sources and Further Reading   85

Index   91

Illustrations

1. Boott millyard on *Sidney & Neff* map of Lowell, 1850   6

2. Bird's-eye map of Lowell, 1876   8

3. Jackhammer archaeology   10

4. Boardinghouse wall revealed   14

5. Probate inventory of Amanda Fox   20

6. Resident Blanche Graham with Mary Beaudry
   and Kathleen Bond   22

7. Recovered plate fragments   24

8. Whiteware coffee cup   25

9. Evening primrose pollen grain   28

10. Goldenrod/aster-type pollen grain   29

11. Laboratory analysis of ceramic fragments   33

12. "Patucket Farms in the Town of Chelmsford," 1822   40

13. Lowell in 1825   41

14. Bird's-eye view of Lowell, 1876   41
15. Kirk Street agents' house today   42
16. Elevations of "one of the . . . Boarding Houses," 1836   43
17. Excavated rear yard of tenement.   45
18. Plan of excavated rear yard   46
19. Sketch of interior of the John Street boardinghouse   50
20. Floor plans and elevations for boardinghouses, 1836   51
21. Washday in a boardinghouse backlot   54
22. "Kiss Me I'm Sterilized" button   56
23. The dining room of a boardinghouse   60
24. Whiteware cup fragments   60
25. Pearlware cup fragments   61
26. Clay pipe with stamped stem   68
27. Embossed pipe bowl   68
28. Illustration of woman smoking a pipe   69
29. One-pint liquor bottles   70
30. Soda bottles   71
31. Liquor bottles found outside a privy   72
32. Copper alloy brooch   76
33. Combs   77
34. Unidentified workers standing outside
    Boott housing, ca. 1889   82

Preface

"Living on the Boott" was a phrase employed by the workers at the Boott Cotton Mills in Lowell, Massachusetts, that came to symbolize a way of life. For those who labored in the mills and then made the short walk to the company-supplied boardinghouses, "the Boott" was both workplace and living accommodation. Throughout much of the nineteenth century, working twelve hours a day, six days a week, skilled and unskilled laborers had little break from their toil in the mills. Their free time was often spent with other workers living in the boardinghouses or, in the case of some skilled workers, with their families in company-supplied tenements. Despite the histories that have been written concerning the industrial revolution and Lowell in particular, there is still much to be learned about the daily lives of mill workers and their world. These people were pivotal actors in one of the most important dramas in human history. Their experiences would contribute to the growth of working-class consciousness and help to form an American culture. Their lives are too important to be left in obscurity. But how do we retrieve them from the past? How do we bring the mill workers and their world back to life so that we can better understand the lives they experienced?

Historical archaeology provides one method for rediscovering these past lives. Unlike the scientists seeking the prehistoric dawn of humankind, historical archaeologists ply their craft filling in the gaps in history. Their search is not for the history of great men or great battles, but for a history rich in texture, full of the lives of ordinary people. Too often, these lives fall below the threshold of a history based solely on the written word. Through excavation, the analysis of artifacts, and a wide range of interdisciplinary techniques, historical archaeologists can weave together the strands of past lives. One of the chief purposes of this book is to explain this process of discovery.

At the heart of this process is our concern for both the people and the world in which they lived. People do not live in a vacuum. Their lives are influenced by the times in which they live. Context gave meaning to people's lives in the past just as today's world gives meaning to our own lives. Language provides a good example of the importance of context. In the 1985 film *Back to the Future*, Michael J. Fox (who goes back in time to the 1950s) often uses the term "heavy" to describe various situations. Doc, his 1950s friend, is perplexed by the term because he assumes it is used literally to mean that things weigh much more in the future. He does not understand the context in which the term was applied. The same is true for archaeologists trying to comprehend the past. Unless we examine the past in its totality, taking into account a full range of evidence, we tend to learn mostly about the lives of wealthy and important persons. This means we need to pay as much attention to the backyard of a boardinghouse inhabited by the working poor as to the biographies written about the influential founders of Lowell. If our goal is a total, more democratic history, both are necessary.

Archaeology is an interdisciplinary field that draws upon diverse disciplines within the social sciences, humanities, and natural sciences, bringing together multiple lines of evidence to examine the cultural and social aspects of material life in the past. Historical archaeology is a subfield of archaeology that focuses on the relatively recent past, employing written records in combination with excavated evidence as primary source materials and using written histories, oral testimony, and pictorial evidence in conjunction with artifact analysis and environmental reconstruction to frame contexts for interpretation. Historians have approached Lowell's past from many angles and from the perspective of many disciplines and subdisciplines: labor history, business and economic history, women's studies, immigration history, the history of technology, architecture, anthropology, folklore, political science, public administration, urban studies, and so forth. Each perspective brings fresh insight into our understanding of Lowell and its place in American history. Historical archaeology, which relies on the methods and products of many disciplines to produce new ways of looking at life in the past, also has a valid role to play. In this little book, we offer a case study that illustrates some of the contributions historical archaeology is making to the broader study of the city's past, noting that although historical archaeology cannot stand alone as an avenue of investigation, it is a valuable complement to histories based on written records alone.

The archaeological record seldom gives us everything we want. We have to take what we can get. In the case of the Boott Mills boardinghouses the record varies. The written record covers the span of Lowell's history. Our data on the evolution of Lowell's urban landscape, the standing buildings and the streets as well as the wealth of archaeological information locked in the soils, are rich in detail and cover the century as a whole. In terms of artifacts, however, the record is most representative of the last three decades of the 1800s and in particular the period at the end of the century. In telling the story that the archaeology reveals, we have tried to minimize the confusion that could arise from moving between these different periods of time, while attempting to maintain the flow of our narrative.

For the same reason, we chose not to interrupt the text with citations and references that might prove distracting; instead, the reader will find at the end of the book a list of sources for each chapter, for in-depth reading on specific points as well as for further, more general exploration of the topics we address.

Many people deserve credit for making this book possible. Most important are the members and staff of the Lowell Historic Preservation Commission who provided funds and direction for the project. In particular we would like to thank Peter Aucella, executive director of the Commission; Peter Promutico, contracting officer for the Commission; and especially Cultural Affairs Officer Juliet Mofford, who provided help, encouragement, and editorial assistance throughout the project as well as patience and understanding. Others who played a role in the Lowell Project were Francis P. McManamon, who was chief of cultural resources for the North Atlantic Region of the National Park Service when the project began, and Myra Harrison, who served in the same capacity when the idea of the book was formulated. She also deserves special thanks for her continuing support of the project as a member of the Lowell Historic Preservation Commission. So many of the staff at the Lowell Historical National Park deserve acknowledgment that we are sure to miss some; however, we would like to thank Chrysandra Walter and Larry Gall for their support of the project. Michael Wurm, Martin Blatt, and Mark Bograd all read portions of the manuscript and for this we thank them. Their comments and suggestions proved vital in seeing the book to completion. Other reviewers included John Worrell of Old Sturbridge Village; James Krowlikowski, who teaches high school in Manchester, New Hampshire, one of New England's great mill towns; and Robert Paynter of the University of Massachusetts, Amherst. Special thanks to Mark Vagos, who was always helpful in the field. Anne Lang and Jane McKinney have helped to edit the final version and Leslie Driscoll has helped with the graphics. Gregory Brown of the Colonial Williamsburg Foundation handled the production of the final text. To the many Boston University graduate students who participated in the Lowell project, thank you for your efforts and enthusiasm. Thanks also to our friend and colleague, Gerald Kelso, whose knowledge of palynology and the landscape was one of the keys to the project's success. To all these and any we have forgotten, thank you.

Living on the Boott

Introduction

Lowell is located at the confluence of the Merrimack and Concord Rivers in northern Massachusetts, near the New Hampshire border. Like most of New England at the beginning of the nineteenth century, this part of Massachusetts, then known as East Chelmsford, was farmland. By the second quarter of the nineteenth century, however, many New England towns were already in transition from agriculture and household manufacture to industrialization and the consumption of shop- and factory-made goods. East Chelmsford was no exception; its location near the falls of the Merrimack and its recently completed power canal for a variety of local factory and milling operations made it an ideal site for the Boston Associates, a group of wealthy investors led by the canny merchant-manufacturer Nathan Appleton, to develop for the expansion of operations beyond the limited capacity of their first mechanized factory in Waltham, Massachusetts.

1

The founding of Lowell in 1825 was a planned venture shaped by the needs of industry and the interests of capital. The factories, street layout, and worker accommodations were constructed according to detailed plans, carefully thought out; in like manner, company regulations promulgated a policy of corporate paternalism intended to guide and protect the morals of workers. The Boston Associates were motivated by the negative model of industrial cities of Europe; they sought to create a total, planned industrial community, to deter the growth of crowded, unsanitary slums for which they might be blamed as much as to avoid conditions that might lead to labor unrest. Initially, the corporations sought to attract young women from New England farms to serve as the unskilled labor force for the mills. The Yankee "mill girls," as they were called, lived in closely supervised, company-run boardinghouses only a short distance from the mills. By day, in red-brick factories stretched along the growing network of power canals, the mill girls tended rank upon rank of water-powered machines that wove millions of yards of cloth. Beyond the mills, a commercial district and residential neighborhoods took shape in a less orderly fashion. By the middle of the nineteenth century, East Chelmsford had been transformed from a farming community boasting some fifty families to a "spindle city" of more than twenty thousand residents, many of whom lived in boardinghouses and tenements.

By midcentury, however, the Yankee "mill girls" were being replaced by immigrant workers, at first Irish and French Canadian. As the nineteenth century progressed, new waves of emigrants from eastern Europe moved to Lowell and took up the unskilled jobs in the mills. Corporate paternalism, the policy intended to safeguard the moral character and physical well-being of young women factory workers, eroded as the work force changed and immigrant workers, often in family groups, predominated as boardinghouse residents. Increasingly, the corporations found that maintaining housing for its labor force was too great a drain on resources, and they began to invest in ways to improve the efficiency of machines and people.

Toward the end of the century, the mills began to sell off housing to private landlords and to demolish boardinghouses to make way for warehouses and other structures. In the twentieth century, organized labor made strikes an effective tool for improving working conditions and pay, but the price proved too high for industrialists to bear. The New England textile economy went into decline as manufacturers relocated to places where labor was cheap and unions were weak.

Today Lowell has emerged from decline and deterioration to serve as the home for new industries and high technology. Much of Lowell's rebirth stems from its people's determination to extol the city's past and from its continuing growth as a diverse, multicultural community, demonstrating that its greatest resources have always been its people and the stories of their lives. The city has memorialized its history and its people in numerous ways: with scholarly and popular books, museum exhibits, parks, festivals, and, as we shall see, archaeological research that highlights and celebrates Lowell's workers and their diverse experiences.

A great deal has been written about Lowell, its place in industrial history, the technological developments of its textile mills, and even about its workers and managers. There is an abundance of historical material from which to gather information, including the stories, letters, and diaries of the workers themselves. But these records, as rich as they are, can only give us one side of the story, that which the people themselves chose to tell in words. There is yet another story buried beneath the streets, parking lots, and yards of present-day Lowell. With the tools and skills of the archaeologist, we can retrieve the story of the everyday lives of workers in Lowell. We can do this by looking at the objects they left behind and the physical world they inhabited.

This book presents the results of the archaeological investigations undertaken by the National Park Service and the Center for Archaeological Studies at Boston University at the request of the Lowell Historic Preservation Commission. This research focused on the mill workers, those people who ran the mills but who have remained in the background of traditional industrial archaeology. The purpose of the research was to illuminate the everyday lives of these people outside the workplace and in their homes, which were, for the most part, the corporation-run boardinghouses and tenements. (The term boardinghouse commonly refers to both the units for unskilled laborers and the tenements for skilled laborers and their families. Throughout the text the term boardinghouse will be employed to refer to both forms of housing except when noted.)

The Boott Mills and Its Boardinghouses

The Boott Cotton Mills was incorporated on March 27, 1835, for the manufacture of cotton and woolen cloth. Housing for mill workers was supplied by the corporation and was only a short walk from the mills. This housing consisted of thirty-two boardinghouses originally designed for unskilled, unmarried workers, and thirty-two tenements (more like apartments) for supervisors or skilled laborers and their families. These units were arranged in eight long blocks, each with four boardinghouses and four tenements.

Tenements were much like apartments or independent living units with individual kitchen facilities. These were the places where families lived. The boardinghouses were very different. They were designed as low-cost communal living units for about thirty people. The person in charge of the boardinghouse was employed by the Boott Mills Corporation and called a "keeper." Housing costs, including board, were deducted from wages. On average, an unskilled laborer received $1.50 to $2.00 per week above the fee of $1.25 to $1.50 deducted for room and board. For this the laborers got cooked meals, washed linens, and a bed, which they sometimes had to share. There were several categories of unskilled and skilled workers and the salaries varied according to the responsibilities and capabilities required for the job. Wages changed over time and were also affected by profits. If profits dropped so did wages.

The primary focus of our research was the unskilled mill workers who lived in the company-owned boardinghouses and the skilled laborers and their families who lived in the adjoining tenements. Excavations were conducted in the yard behind boardinghouse unit #45 as well as in the yard of tenement unit #48 in the building block along James (later Sirk) Street. This was one of eight boardinghouse blocks that the Boott Mills constructed between 1835 and 1839. Historical research before excavation gave us a fairly good idea of who had lived there.

In order to provide a point of comparison we also conducted excavations in the rear yard of the Kirk Street agents' house, which was constructed in 1845. This was the house in which the agents for the Boott and Massachusetts Cotton Mills lived. The agent served a function similar to the chief executive officer of a major company today. He was hired by the owners of the mills to run the mills. This was a multifaceted task that included everything from overseeing the construction of the mills to supervising company personnel. The comparison of the ordinary workers' backyards and the agents' backyard highlighted aspects of nineteenth-century life such as diet, land use, and disease that may not have been obvious otherwise.

Boardinghouse Residents

There is some information recorded about the residents of Boott units #45 and #48, but since the personal lives of employees were not considered important, the information is rather vague. Workers came and went, but usually only their names, ages, and sometimes their places of birth were recorded.

Boardinghouse unit #45 was inhabited almost exclusively by women from 1850 through 1880 (usually around twenty-five to thirty women at any given time) while it was under the control of one keeper, Amanda Fox. Letters from former tenants and Boott Company correspondence paint Amanda as a hard-working widow who took her responsibilities as a keeper seriously. The character of the boardinghouse changed after Amanda's death. Censuses from 1900 and

1. The view (looking west) of Boott millyard shown on the Sidney & Neff 1850 map of Lowell. (Courtesy of Lowell Historical Society.)

1910 show that the house was occupied then almost entirely by men, the majority of whom were French Canadian in 1910. Also, in 1910 the house was no longer overseen by a woman, but by Joseph Croteau. We shall examine this population change later.

The tenement, unit #48, had a very different occupation history. From at least 1850 through 1900 it housed a series of families, all of which included small children. In the censuses, the men were listed as skilled workers in the mill and their wives kept house.

The boardinghouses and tenements along James Street were sold by the Boott Mills Corporation into private hands sometime around 1907. They were turned into private rental units, though the tenants continued to be mill employees. Both units #45 and #48 ceased to be used as dwellings by 1918, and were turned into storage facilities instead. The entire block was torn down in 1934, after which it was used as a coal yard and then as a parking lot.

A more personal view of the boardinghouses is offered by the oral history of a woman who lived in one as a child in the early part of this century. Blanche Pelletier Graham lived in a Boott Mills boarding-house on John Street (one block over from the boardinghouse we excavated) from 1907 to 1912. Because Blanche was a child when she lived on John Street, she had the memories of a child, not those of an adult mill worker. But she was able to remember the layout of the house she lived in and even to make a sketch of the first floor. She remembered helping the keeper set and clear the table at meal times, and that the meals were hearty. She slept in a bed with her sister in the same room as their parents, and played in the mill yard and along the canals using spools and rusty wheels as props for playing house.

The Boardinghouse Backyards
Maps and building plans from the nineteenth century show the yards only as spaces; we have no other information detailing their appearance. The backyards of the Boott boardinghouse block along James Street seem to have been designed for utilitarian purposes. The maps show a one-story wooden shed that ran the entire length of the block

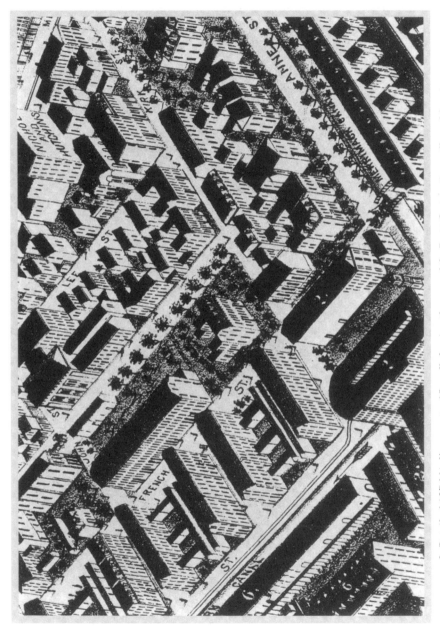

2. Detail of 1876 bird's-eye map of Lowell showing the area of the Boott Corporation mills and housing.

and separated the yards from the alley behind. We assumed that in this shed were privies (outhouses) for each housing unit and storage spaces for firewood.

At some point, probably by around 1876, additions were made to the houses to connect them with their sheds so that people could get to the privies without going outside. After about 1900 the privies were filled in with dirt and replaced by water closets inside the boarding-houses themselves. The sheds were converted for use as coal stores and trash receptacles. Backyard wells supplied the buildings' residents with water. Public water was available to Boott properties as early as 1873, but some units relied on well water into the 1890s.

We know that the yards were used by all residents until about 1900, as long as the privies were housed in the back sheds. Although very little is known about the specific appearance of the yards of Boott Mills units #45 and #48 and what activities went on there, photographs of other boardinghouses and tenements provide an idea. These photographs depict utilitarian spaces put to multiple uses. Among the washtubs, scattered trash, and plank walkways children might play as their mothers worked. While the yards in the photographs are notable for their disarray, there are nonetheless touches of decoration such as flowerboxes in windows overlooking the clotheslines.

Archaeology in a Parking Lot

There was no hint that a block-long, three-story building once stood on what is now the parking lot we were to excavate. The building was razed in 1934 and the lot was paved. Along one side of the parking lot, an identical building recently restored still stands, so we knew what the original building looked like. There was, however, little information about what the yards looked like or how they were used. In order to pry the secrets of the boardinghouses' backyards from the ground, we first had to confront some of the problems inherent in urban archaeology. What can an archaeologist do when a site is cov-

3. Jackhammer archaeology: removing blacktop from Boott Mills'
parking lot before excavation.

ered with asphalt? Not only did the parking lot hide any evidence of
a boardinghouse block or its backyard, but a sea of cars hid much of
the parking lot. Since the lot was in active use during our initial excavations, we were limited to eight parking spaces. This meant that we
had to conform our excavations to the dimensions of these spaces.
We could not tailor the size or shape of our excavation units to any
expected remains. This limitation did not affect the success of the initial operation, however, because we were able to determine precisely
where to dig by carefully studying a map made in 1892 for insurance
purposes. This map, matched to existing reference points, allowed us
to establish the exact location of the demolished boardinghouses and
their backyards.

The first phase of excavation was simply a test to determine how
intact and how extensive the boardinghouse remains were. The exca-

vation units were marked out on the parking lot with spray paint, and a jackhammer removed the asphalt. Directly below the cinder and sand parking lot bedding, we encountered the expected remains of the boardinghouses and their outbuildings.

Encouraged by these immediate results, we were able to focus on two specific backyards, those of Boardinghouse #48 and Tenement #45. We stripped off the blacktop from both yards, and after some careful cleaning and excavation, we exposed the yards to view. From above, they looked much as they probably did in the early part of this century, after the buildings had been torn down.

Once the yards were exposed, we carefully set about the task of excavating them layer by layer and exploring the many features we encountered, such as building foundations, filled-in wells, outhouse pits, and old planting holes. Each of these had to be measured, drawn, and photographed as part of the recording process that is the heart of any archaeological project. This type of detail is necessary to reconstruct the different periods of use. Some features are found above or below others, and recording this helps us to understand their temporal relationship. Another important part of the archaeological process is the collection of samples for later analysis. Soils from features such as planting holes or drains can be investigated using a variety of techniques that will be discussed in more detail in the chapter that follows. Without the recording of the locations of artifacts and features and the collection of soil samples for analysis, our picture of the past would be an imprecise, impressionistic image rather than the controlled, richly detailed portrait that is created by using the techniques of historical archaeology.

We uncovered a wealth of information, mostly from the period toward the end of the 1800s. This was a time when the mills employed more foreign-born workers than they did at the beginning of the century. At the same time the company began selling some of the boardinghouses. The boardinghouse that we investigated was sold to Saimon Sirk, thus ending company control and upkeep.

These are important facts to keep in mind while considering different aspects of life in the corporation-run housing. But before we try to pull together the pieces of information excavated from the Boott Mills backyards, we should explore the nature of archaeological research and examine the different tools an archaeologist uses to reconstruct the past.

Historical Archaeology in Context

People always want to know what kind of "good stuff" archaeologists have found, but archaeologists are not primarily interested in finding objects of beauty or value. To an archaeologist, everything from charred bone to microscopic remains of food is potentially exciting and informative. Objects alone cannot tell us very much about the past; it is only through their context that we can learn something. A ceramic vessel on a museum shelf is meaningless unless we know where it came from and in what context it was found. The vessel need not be beautiful or valuable in order to have meaning; a few sherds of plain pottery in a grave tell us that people were buried with grave goods, which in turn tells us something about the belief system of the culture to which the person belonged.

A burial is a form of archaeological context, but it is also a cultural context. By cultural context we mean what people thought

4. Blacktop removed revealing boardinghouse wall remains.

about the time in which they lived: their opinions or their beliefs. The phrase also refers to people's preferences for certain kinds of food or clothing, or their behaviors like smoking or drinking. The physical environment in which people lived is also important to archaeologists, whether we are studying the climate of a region or the specific conditions that existed in someone's backyard. Another important aspect of context is social class. Consider three different housing sites: an abandoned city lot, weed-infested and littered with debris; a narrow urban house lot with an elongated, narrow townhouse and small front garden, tiny but well tended; the carefully groomed and expansive lawn of the White House. Each context has different meanings, and the appearance of each is a measure of the regard owners, residents, caretakers, or taxpayers have for the property and the social standing of the owners or residents. All these factors contributed to form the context that gave meaning to people's lives in the past. This is why so much archaeological research is concerned with trying to reconstruct and understand context.

An effective way to get the most out of an archaeological investigation is to use every kind of evidence available. Historical archaeologists use many of the same tools that prehistoric archaeologists use, but they can go further by incorporating elements of written and spoken history into their investigations. They have wider sources because historical archaeologists study time periods for which written records exist. The same can be said of industrial archaeology, which focuses on the remains, above and below ground, of industry and on the material evidence for the history of technology. Historical archaeology focuses on people and culture, and complements industrial archaeology when it is applied to the examination of the domestic lives of workers. The following section presents some of the methods that we use to illuminate the lives of everyday people living in the past.

Tools of the Trade

The following list is not meant to be exhaustive, but rather a sample of the range of tools that the historical archaeologist relies on. All these tools played an important part in our investigations in Lowell.

Excavation

Excavation is the activity that defines archaeology as a way of learning about the past and distinguishes it from digging in the ground for any other reason. Archaeological excavation is the systematic examination of features such as foundations, post holes, wells, and so forth and of artifacts, plant and animal remains, and other evidence contained in site soils in relationship to the soil layers in which they occur. Sites are formed by both human and natural actions, and each kind of activity leaves clues of some sort, although some are faint and difficult to decipher without scientific procedures, a number of which we describe below. The way an archaeologist approaches a site depends on a variety of factors, including the kind of site it is, where it is located, the questions the archaeologist would like to answer through excavation, and the amount of time and money available for the work. There are nevertheless some very basic characteristics of any archaeological excavation.

Archaeologists first divide up a site into a grid, a series of units or "squares," the corners of which are precisely located in space. Working within one grid unit at a time, the excavators remove soil carefully, in gradual increments. For the most part, excavation requires patience and a good eye for changes in the soil; archaeologists take care to observe and record information about changes in the color, texture, and composition (e.g., sand, silt, gravel) of soil layers. They also pay close attention to what they find in order to interpret what went on in different parts of a site (Was there a fire here? Is this where they butchered a cow? Was this a garden, a trash dump, an old path, or just a pack rat's nest?) and to establish the chronology or sequence in which the soil layers were formed.

Archaeology is a term often used to describe other sorts of studies that involve taking things apart systematically, recording everything as the process of dismantling the evidence proceeds. Architectural historians, for instance, practice a kind of "architectural archaeology" when they examine the construction history of a house by exposing layers of paint or wallpaper, removing wall coverings to find closed-up windows and doors, and so on. There is a dramatic difference between this sort of above-ground archaeology and below-ground excavation, however. Just like the archaeologist, the architectural historian keeps careful records and numbers the architectural pieces as they are removed, but a house can be restored or reconstructed. Once a site is excavated, *even when this has been done systematically and carefully*, it can never be reassembled or reconstructed—except through the records kept by archaeologists.

For this reason you will find many people on an archaeological site taking notes, writing up their observations and ideas about what they are finding and what it might mean, and making scale drawings on graph sheets. They record, for example, plans of the "floors" of the excavation units as each new level is exposed or they sketch profiles of the walls of units to illustrate the soil layers exactly as they appear. Archaeologists also take photographs in black and white and color at every stage of an excavation; some use video cameras as yet another way of recording everything that is uncovered. More and more archaeologists are turning to computers in the field, using laptops for keeping notes and laser transits to record the exact positions of their finds so that later they can feed the data into a powerful computer to generate precise maps of where things were found. Some computer programs permit an archaeologist to produce a three-dimensional representation of a site—the closest we can ever get to putting a site back together again!

The excavations we describe here both took place in 1986. At the boardinghouse's backlots a crew of eight worked for five weeks in late fall, assisted by many volunteers, many of whom were students in an introductory archaeology class at Boston University. At the Kirk Street site of the duplex that housed agents for the Boott and Massachusetts Mills, we spent two weeks in the summer of 1986 with a crew of four. At the agents' house we excavated a row of six 2 m. x 2 m. units and two units each 1 m. x 2 m. in size at the back of the lot assigned to the agent of the Massachusetts Mills; at the boardinghouse site, we excavated two huge areas, each 10 m. x 12 m., exposing the backlots in their entirety. We found no features in the agents' backlot that were not of recent date, but the boardinghouse's backlots contained features such as drains, privies, wells, and foundations that covered the entire period of the housing for workers at the Boott Mills. In addition to these features, we recovered food remains in the form of animal bones and plant parts, fragments of glass and pottery eating and drinking vessels, clay smoking pipes, corroded nails, thousands of pieces of broken window glass (one unit had more than 7000 pieces in a single soil layer!), and various small, personal items that people lost or threw away in the backlots, including buttons, beads, hair combs, pins, jewelry, and collar studs.

For every week in the field, we spent three to five weeks in the lab, cleaning, cataloging, and analyzing all of the finds. We also spent a great deal of time examining original documents that helped us to interpret our site and learn about the people who lived there.

Documents

One of the major differences between historical and prehistoric archaeology is that historical archaeologists often can put names and faces on the people they are studying. Historical archaeologists have a good chance of acquainting themselves with the people they are studying by looking at the records in which their names appear and at the paintings, drawings, and photographs that depict them. We can talk about the events in someone's life, and sometimes actually observe the very objects that this person made or used and left behind. In this way, the work of historical archaeologists can take on personal and biographical dimensions, making the experience of the past even more immediate for us.

When archaeologists talk about documents they are referring to written records, usually those that were produced during the time period being studied. Documents come in many forms, not just published sources such as books, newspapers, and magazines, but also unpublished records such as letters, personal financial accounts, or property deeds.

Personal documents include letters, diaries, and memoirs in which people recorded their thoughts and feelings about the private events of their lives. Embedded in them are clues about the values and social mores of the time. Usually the researcher looks beyond the literal statements about facts or events in these documents and tries to "interrogate" the source, using corroborative or contradictory information from other sources to determine the writer's accuracy, veracity, and perhaps what his or her unspoken assumptions were.

Other documents are less personal, more official records of events, transactions, or accounts. Examples include tax records, property deeds, census reports, and court records. While these documents can also have cultural clues embedded in them, they contain apparently objective information about population demographics, including details about people's finances, property ownership, and legal problems. Since these documents are often standardized (for a given area at a given point in time), they can be used to answer questions about whole groups of people.

One of the things that a historical archaeologist is trained to do is to read documents critically, to know what questions they can answer, and what the limitations of the various documents are. A brief discussion of one kind of document—the probate inventory—will serve as an example of how an archaeologist might make use of the written record.

"Probate" is the legal term used to describe a host of activities that are carried out at the time a person dies in order to manage and dispose of personal property. One element of probate is an inventory of the person's assets, including the movable household items. In this country today, only the total monetary value of the estate is usually recorded. Up until the end of the 1800s, however, probate inventories were very detailed, often listing a person's belongings room by room and item by item. When you read such an inventory you can imagine

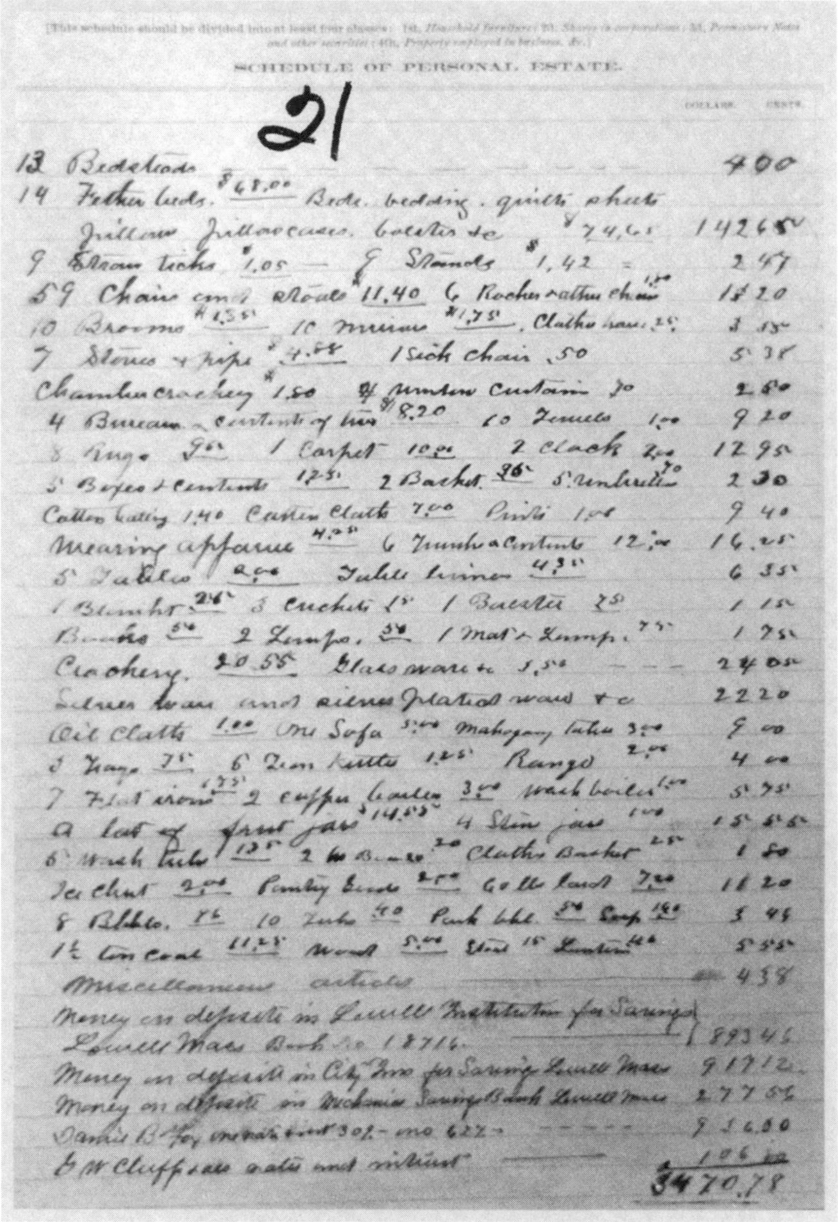
[This schedule should be divided into at least four classes: 1st, Household furniture; 2d, Shares in corporations; 3d, Promissory Notes and other securities; 4th, Property employed in business, &c.]

SCHEDULE OF PERSONAL ESTATE.

DOLLARS. CENTS.

21

13 Bedsteads 4 00
14 Feather beds $68.00 Beds, bedding, quilts, sheets pillows, pillowcases, bolsters &c $74.65 142 65
9 Straw ticks $1.05 — 9 Stands $1.42 = 2 47
59 Chairs and stools $11.40 6 Rocker rattan chairs 1.80 13 20
10 Brooms $1.35 10 mirrors $1.75, Clothes horses .25 3 35
7 Stoves + pipe $4.88 1 Sick chair .50 5 38
Chamber crockery $1.80 4 window curtains .80 2 60
4 Bureaus + contents of them $8.20 10 Towels 1.00 9 20
8 Rugs .95 1 Carpet 10.00 2 Clocks 2.00 12 95
5 Boxes + contents 1.25 2 Baskets .25 5 Umbrellas .70 2 30
Cotton batting 1.40 Cotton cloth 7.00 Prints 1.00 9 40
Wearing apparel 4.25 6 Trunks + contents 12.00 16.25
5 Tables 2.00 Table linen 4.35 6 35
1 Blankets .25 3 Crickets .15 1 Basket .75 1 15
Books .50 2 Lamps .50 1 Mat + Lamp .75 1 75
Crockery 20.55 Glassware &c 3.50 — — 24 05
Silver ware and silver plated ware &c 22 20
Oil cloth 1.00 One Sofa 5.00 Mahogany table 3.00 9 00
3 Trays .75 6 Iron kettles 1.25 Range 2.00 4 00
7 Flat irons .75 2 copper boilers 3.00 wash boiler 1.00 5 75
A lot of fruit jars $14.55 4 Stone jars 1.00 15 55
6 Wash tubs 1.35 2 Brooms .20 Clothes basket .25 1 80
Ice chest 2.00 Poultry house 2.00 60 lbs lard 7.20 11 20
8 Bbls. .76 10 Tubs .40 Pork bbl. .50 Soap 1.80 3 46
1½ ton coal 11.25 Wood 5.00 Stool .15 Lantern .10 5 55
Miscellaneous articles 4 38
Money on deposit in Lowell Institution for Savings Lowell Mass Book No 18716 893 46
Money on deposit in City Ins for Savings Lowell Mass 917 12
Money on deposit in Mechanics Savings Bank Lowell Mass 277 56
Daniel B. Fox one note [illegible] 30% — no 622 — — — — — 935 00
G W Cliff's sale note and interest 106 00
3470.78

5. *Probate inventory of Amanda Fox.*

the recorder walking through the house with pen and paper in hand, examining each object carefully, counting candlesticks, chairs, and spoons, and finally assigning a monetary value to each possession. One can easily imagine the value of such a listing to archaeologists. Not only can researchers ascertain the objects a person possessed, but they can also learn the colloquial names for these objects. What is more significant, researchers can determine the very room in which a given object was used or at least stored. In this way we can get an idea of how people organized their space, and hence, how their lives differed from or were similar to our own.

Figure 5 shows the probate inventory of Amanda Fox's boarding-house, made shortly after her death in 1895. Although the handwriting is difficult to read, the transcription shows what kinds of items were in the house.

As compelling and evocative as a detailed probate inventory is, these records do not provide us with everything. For one thing, the listing is usually not very descriptive. An entry might read "6 dinner plates," but what kind? Were they fancy and expensive, or plain, durable, and inexpensive? Were they in good condition and treated as treasured objects, or were they chipped and treated carelessly? Did the six plates match, or were there different colors and designs? Another problem with probate inventories is that not everyone who died had an estate large enough to require one. Only people with a significant amount of property were inventoried. The poorest members of society had nothing of monetary value to pass on, so inventories were unnecessary. This discrepancy creates a serious distortion in the historical record, and one that the researcher who is interested in all classes of people in a culture cannot ignore. A probate inventory, like many other kinds of documents, is therefore only one source of information. It can provide a starting point for our inquiry and a backdrop for the materials that are excavated, but documents are not enough. They are just one component in a wide array of resources available to the historical archaeologist.

6. Former boardinghouse resident Blanche Graham describes her life on the Boott to Mary Beaudry (center) and Kathleen Bond (left).

Oral Histories

Although the documentary record is composed of history that has been written down, oral history is the history that has been remembered by living people. Oral histories are the verbal analogies of personal documents. They are narrated recollections of people, usually in the form of tape recorded interviews, and contain valuable information about the specific time period and place being investigated by the archaeologist. An oral history can also derive from a series of informal conversations and oral histories are now sometimes recorded on film or video. The primary advantage of an oral history is that it provides a personal and interesting picture of the past. There are some drawbacks, however. First, oral histories are limited to the relatively recent past—essentially the length of a lifetime. Oral histories recorded by earlier researchers are sometimes available, but these too can be frustrating if the kinds of questions asked by the interviewer differ from those of interest to the current researcher. The biggest drawback, however, is the very quality that makes oral histories so interesting: their subjectivity. People's memories are notoriously inaccurate, and facts uncovered in an oral history usually require independent corroboration. Just as researchers must read between the lines of a personal document, they must learn to look beneath the surface of an oral history and ferret out its cultural significance.

Features

Nonportable material remains such as building foundations, wells, graves, and landscaping elements are referred to as features. Archaeologists give special attention to features because they are so highly informative about cultural practices and social life. Architectural features such as postholes, foundations, and cellar holes reveal the sorts of houses people lived in and the kinds of public buildings or spaces they used for worship, commerce, or manufacturing. The relationship among features—their layout in space— is evidence of social structure and class distinctions.

Other features reflect the ways in which people responded to basic needs and changing technology. Installations for waste and water management and other utilities are very revealing about conditions of sanitation and hygiene and overall quality of life. Many features became receptacles for refuse and debris once they no longer served their original purpose. Archaeologists can learn a great deal from the discarded objects they find in abandoned wells, privies, borrow pits (holes dug to find clay or gravel), cellars, and the like. They take special care to record the profile or vertical sequence of deposition in such features so they can interpret how long a feature performed its original function before it was used for the disposal of wastes, how long it took to fill it, and exactly when and why this process took place. Often it is possible to link the remains with specific families or households living at a site and to determine whether

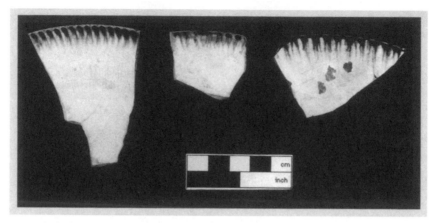

7. Blue-edged whiteware plate fragments recovered from boardinghouse yard.

the artifacts from the deposit were thrown away because a widow disposed of things once belonging to her husband, or a new wife chose to get rid of unpleasant reminders of her predecessor, or simply that moving day was the occasion for a very thorough job of housecleaning!

Artifacts

Artifacts are the traditional source of information that archaeologists rely on to interpret the past. In simplest terms, artifacts are the material objects that humans make, buy, use, discard, or lose during their lifetimes. In the archaeologist's vocabulary, artifacts are usually those objects that are portable, such as stone tools, ceramic dishes, jewelry, and building materials. Because the study of artifacts is so often misunderstood by nonarchaeologists, let us look at one of the most common artifacts recovered from archaeological sites: ceramics.

Ceramics figure prominently in the preparation, storage, and serving of food. By examining the types of ceramic vessels found at a site, the archaeologist can learn about the basic dietary patterns and dining habits of the inhabitants. One aspect of our analysis of ceramics from the Boott Corporation housing involved a comparison of the types of vessels found in deposits behind the tenement for skilled workers and their families with the types of vessels from the board-inghouse deposits. The differences that we discovered were subtle. For example we found that supervisors' families purchased and used a greater variety of dishes intended for the individual diner, such as bread plates. This discovery led us, in turn, to the conclusion that supervisors' wives tried to maintain the values of family life by setting their tables according to contemporary notions of appropriate dining customs. At the boardinghouse, there was little evidence of refine-ments of this sort. Here communal dining was suggested by the assortment of serving bowls and platters intended to contain large quantities of food. There was nothing to indicate individually pre-sented servings or other niceties that went along with the socially charged character of nineteenth-century formal dining. Thus, ceram-ic analysis can reveal the social differences that families and boarders brought to mealtimes.

Apart from what artifacts reveal about cultural practices, everyday

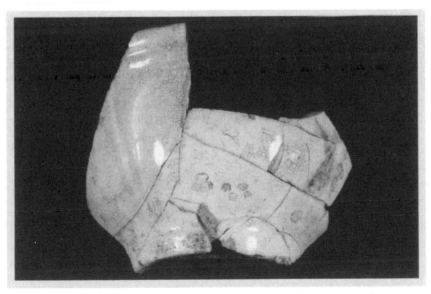

8. Partially reconstructed, plain whiteware coffee cup pieced together from fragments recovered from boardinghouse yard.

behavior, and social differences, they play a critical role in helping archaeologists to assign dates to their sites and to the features and soil layers in them. Styles and tastes change over time, resulting in the introduction of new forms and new types of decoration on objects. Sometimes old ideas and styles are recycled and introduced as new—or maybe even as fashionably "retro." Technological advances over time mean that things are made differently at different periods, often with newly discovered or invented materials. So even "retro" items—Roman copies of Greek statues, for instance, or 1950s clothing styles using Velcro fasteners—provide clues to their actual date of manufacture. Archaeologists employ several lines of evidence in arriving at dates for sites and portions of sites. Prehistoric archaeologists often use scientifically based procedures that measure elapsed time based on ratios of decay of carbon or other unstable materials over thousands of years. Historical archaeologists are sometimes lucky enough to find objects with dates right on them—coins, for example—but this is relatively rare. Usually they reason from information gleaned from written sources in combination with the evidence of where times are found within the site.

For example, at the Lowell boardinghouse site we found hundreds of fragments of white clay smoking pipes, many of which bore lettering naming their city and country of manufacture. By consulting sources on various manufactured goods, we learned that pipes marked with the country of manufacture (in this case Scotland) were made after 1890, when the United States government began to enforce the McKinley Tariff, which imposed taxes on imported goods. Earlier pipe stems were marked with only the city of manufacture or with nothing concerning where they were produced. Thus, even in a tiny object such as a pipe stem archaeologists have a clue to the date of the soil level in which the artifact was found, plus evidence for trade patterns, not to mention smoking habits!

Stratigraphy

Under ideal circumstances, the archaeologist's general rule of thumb is that the oldest things will be found in the deepest layers of a site, where as the newest are near or at the surface. This principle is based on the fact that layers of soil tend to build up and bury anything left on or in an old ground surface. Soil layers are formed from the deterioration of the rocks that make up the natural bedrock of a region, which itself is formed by various geological processes including metamorphosis of the earth's molten core into rock, sedimentation in bodies of water, and volcanic eruptions. The layers take on the characteristics of the parent material and build up over time. But, as we mentioned earlier, both nature and culture tend to intervene in this idealized scheme of things, altering the arrangement of soil layers and the relationships between features and artifacts people may have left behind.

Almost everything that people do as part of taking shelter, getting and eating food, and just going about daily life leaves evidence in some form. They may build fires, butcher animals, gather plants and seeds and convert them into food or useful items, and so on. They are very likely to dig holes in the ground in order to store goods or deposit trash, shelter a fire from the wind, bury a departed relative, construct a house, or mine clay from which they can fashion bricks to build the house. Site stratigraphy, as the interpretation of soil layers is called, involves deciphering the ways in which humans have altered the landscape by adding to and subtracting from the naturally occurring sequence of soil strata in a given locale.

Even after humans have abandoned a site and ceased to have an effect on it, nature continues its work. In addition to long-term geological processes, local and regional natural events such as rodent burrowing, erosion by wind and water, floods, earthquakes, landslides, and frost heave alter the condition of sites and the remains they contain.

People living in prehistoric times had an impact on their environment, to be sure, but at historical sites we often find extreme examples of deliberate manipulation of the environment. In places where people lived for many generations, they often repeatedly dug through accumulated layers of soil and sealed over evidence of previous occupation periods, mixing together the soils and artifacts from earlier times with soils and artifacts from their own. The archaeologist's task is to sort out all of these events and to reconstruct the sequence of deposition and redeposition. The goal, essentially, is to reconstruct the life history of a site.

City dwellers and farmers alike have a tendency to reshape the landscape to suit themselves. At times they create vast amounts of real estate, forming land where once there was none by using soil, trash, building refuse, or a combination of these materials as landfill to reclaim swampy or low-lying areas or even to make new land along shorelines. Landfill can be thought of as an artifact in its own right; in the life history of a site it usually represents a single, massive occurrence rather than a gradual or cumulative series of events.

Plant Remains

People use plants in a variety of ways, not only for food but also as raw material for making useful objects, clothing, and shelter. We can learn a great deal about people by examining the kinds of plants available to them at a given place and time, discovering which ones they used, and understanding how they used them.

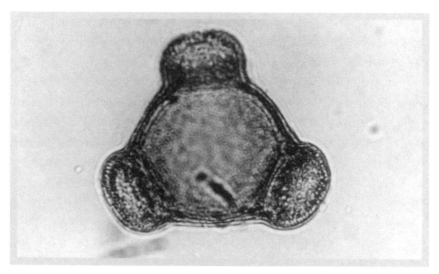

9. Enlargement of evening primrose pollen grain as seen through microscope.

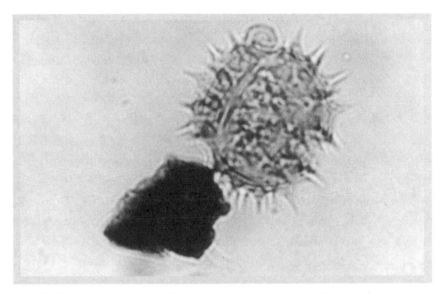

10. Enlargement of goldenrod/aster-type pollen grain as seen through microscope.

Plant remains come in different forms; wood and seeds are most common. The person responsible for their analysis is usually called an archaeobotanist or an ethnobotanist. Wood survives under conditions of extreme wetness or dryness. Some wooden tools, weapons, building materials, and figures that are thousands of years old have been found on archaeological sites. In order for a seed to survive, it usually needs to be charred or recovered from an archaeological feature that contains wet soils, such as a well, a privy, or a drain. In these instances the preservation of even uncharred seeds can sometimes be remarkable. Seeds are a good source of information about what people in different cultures ate, what they grew, and the kind of environment in which they lived.

Pollen
Besides being a nuisance to people with allergies, pollen is an important source of information about plants. Plant pollen that does not make its way to fertilize another plant settles on the ground and

becomes buried over time. Pollen can survive for long periods in this way, and since the pollen of different plants is identifiable under a microscope, a trained specialist, called a palynologist, can determine what plants were part of a particular environment at a given point in time.

Pollen data has mostly been used by researchers to get an idea of what plants were available to people in the natural surroundings where they lived. Pollen moves around in several ways, the most common being on the wind and on the bodies of animals and insects. Wind-borne pollen can travel great distances before it comes to rest, while animal-borne pollen tends to remain closer to home. This means that palynologists must know which plants produce which kind of pollen. Wind-borne pollen gives a *regional* environmental picture, while animal-borne pollen gives more of a *local* environmental picture.

Recent pollen studies have shown that careful analysis can provide detailed and site-specific information about how very local environments such as a single backyard changed over time. Changes in pollen frequencies and rates of deterioration can indicate episodes of landscaping, lawn maintenance, and disuse.

Phytoliths
Phytoliths, the inorganic casts of plant structures, including cells, are another source of information about plants. Soft unstable organic tissues of many living plants can be filled with hard inorganic silicates that are resistant to damage and deterioration. Since the cell shapes of different plants are distinguishable, phytoliths of various plants can be identified. A particular advantage of phytoliths to archaeological research is that they tend to remain precisely where their parent plant died, thus providing extremely localized information. The disadvantage of phytoliths is that they are only identifiable by gross shape, which does not tend to vary between species. This means that only higher taxonomic levels such as families can be distinguished. However, in conjunction with pollen data phytoliths can also be used to reconstruct local environmental events.

Animal Remains

Bones constitute the most common form of animal or faunal remains encountered by archaeologists. Bones are most often the by-products of a meal but they can also be the remains of tools. In some cases they are the mortal remains of pets or pests, or, as is usually the case with human bones, they are what is left from a burial. In a nineteenth-century urban site such as Lowell, the most common bones tend to be from animals that were eaten, domesticated, or disdained, such as rodents. The zooarchaeologists who analyze the animal remains also wish to know what kinds of nonfood animals frequented a place since this information can provide hints regarding how well kept an area was and what kinds of diseases the humans living there were exposed to. But archaeologists pay even more attention to the bones of animals that people consumed. We can learn not only what kinds of meat people ate, but also how they butchered their game and livestock.

One example of how this information can be useful comes from observations concerning the manner in which butchering practices changed in the nineteenth century. Before this, many animal carcasses were butchered by chopping, probably with an ax. Marks left by an ax are usually identifiable. At the very end of the eighteenth century, however, saws began to be used to divide carcasses into manageable sizes.

This change corresponded to a change in the way people ate meals. Before 1800 many people tended to eat stews that combined a mixture of foods and were served in large bowls. In America this custom started to change around the turn of the century as more and more people began eating a variety of cuts of meat. In fact, beef, the mainstay of many American diets, began to be butchered into cuts that are familiar to us today, such as chuck roast.

Parasites

Organisms that live within the bodies of animals (including humans) can leave behind eggs that survive in archaeological soils. The examination of these eggs provides archaeologists with at least two different kinds of information about a site.

First, parasite eggs are present in very dense concentrations only in fecal soils, that is, soils derived from animal or human excrement. This is significant because the interpretation of the eggs themselves—and any other material found in that soil—would be different for fecal and nonfecal soils. Seeds in a fecal deposit, for example, come from plants that the animal ate. Seeds in a nonfecal deposit come from plants that existed in the area and that may or may not have been eaten by the animals living there.

Second, sometimes the kind of organism that inhabited the person or animal can be identified from its egg. Since specific parasites frequent particular animals, we can infer what kinds of animals were present. The identification of parasite eggs provides a glimpse into the state of health and hygiene of the humans living in the area.

Soil Compounds

Although archaeologists tend to focus on cultural remains such as artifacts, they also examine the soil itself for clues to human activity. Not only do humans shape their landscape, leave behind objects that become buried in the earth, and discard food remains, but they also affect the chemical and physical properties of the soil itself. Phosphorus is one chemical that occurs in higher concentrations in places where humans and animals have lived than it does naturally. Most phosphorus produced by humans comes from urine, feces, trash, food, and dead bodies. This means that high levels of phosphorus in the soil may be used to identify places, where garbage has been deposited or where animals were kept.

Analysis of soils at the boardinghouses produced strikingly high readings of lead in the soil, possibly from the use of lead paint. Lead, then, could have contributed to the overall deterioration in worker health noted by late nineteenth-century reformers.

11. Laboratory analysis of ceramic fragments unearthed in boardinghouse backyards.

Putting the Pieces Together

There are two broad stages of all archaeological investigations: the actual gathering of data through excavation and other fieldwork; and the analysis, which includes the processing and synthesis of the data in the laboratory. The analysis phase normally takes far longer than the excavation. At first the specialists work individually. Soil samples are distributed to the various scientists whose evidence is literally suspended in the dirt. The soil specialist measures the chemical components of the soils; the palynologist and phytolith expert extract their evidence from soil samples; the archaeobotanist separates seeds and other plant remains from the soil by flotation. This process involves immersing the soil sample in water and skimming off the plant remains that float to the top while others are caught in very fine meshed screens. Pollen, phytoliths, and seeds then are identified and counted under a microscope. The zooarchaeologist uses a comparative collection to identify the animal bones and studies the butchery marks on them.

At the same time, laboratory technicians process the artifacts by cleaning all of the finds and labeling them with numbers that identify exactly where they were found on the site. Then each artifact is cataloged. The catalog entry includes information about what the object is (a fragment of the stem of a white clay pipe, for instance), its distinctive characteristics (for example, embossed lettering along the stem that reads "Glasgow Scotland"), and manufacturing information about when the item might have been made.

After each item is cataloged, the information is placed into a computer, which stores the data. Computers are an essential part of any archaeological project. They not only store many of the often hundreds of thousands of pieces of information gathered from the analysis of the artifacts, but they also provide the means to analyze the information. The result can be something as simple as a chart or a graph that records the number of ceramics found on a site, or as complicated as a map of the horizontal distribution of artifacts that illustrates where specific activities took place on a site. Although computers are not absolutely necessary to carry out this kind of spatial analysis, the computer provides the best tool for the archaeologist to manage, analyze, and display many thousands of pieces of information. By plotting where things were found on the site, we learn about patterns of rubbish disposal as well as patterns of other activities in different areas the site.

The analysis does not stop with the computer, however. Often artifacts of special interest, such as ceramics, glass, tobacco pipes, and so forth, are grouped together for more detailed analysis. This procedure can involve piecing together the broken fragments of ceramic or glass vessels so that what is called a "minimum vessel count" can be made. In this way, it is possible to figure out from the fragments how many actual vessels existed originally. Knowing the number of vessels that were collected on a site, as well as their sizes and shapes, tells us a great deal about drinking habits and consumer patterns of the people who lived there. After all, people used whole objects, not fragments!

This sort of detailed study also involves further research into documents and books about objects and how they were used. The ultimate aim of all this painstaking artifact analysis—all the washing, counting, sorting, and reconstructing carried on by individual specialists—is to be able to place the objects back into their cultural context so that historical archaeologists can understand how people used them in their daily lives.

In the final phase of analysis, all of the specialists sit down with the archaeologists and exchange ideas about what they think their findings mean. Often this exchange is an on-going process that takes place during periodic meetings of the project team in which results of the individual analyses are discussed to see where data agree or, in some cases, conflict. This collaboration is the essence of interdisciplinary research, and often this phase of the project is the most exciting because, essentially, everyone becomes an archaeologist. Frequently, areas needing further research may be apparent and, more likely than not, preliminary interpretations based on only one type of analysis will have to be revised. Interdisciplinary research is an interactive effort. A truly thorough and reliable interpretation of any site comes from the interchange of ideas among all the specialists who have participated in the project.

Archaeology at the Boott Mills

The archaeological investigations at the Boott Mills in Lowell used all of the sources of information described above to form what is called an interdisciplinary study. Together, the collection and analysis of these various forms of data allowed us to reconstruct aspects of people's lives in the past. For the Lowell project this meant conveying a picture of life as experienced by workers in an industrial city of the late 1800s. We wanted to understand how the people who ran the industrial machinery structured their lives and shaped their world. We know that many aspects of their lives were programmed for them by their powerful and influential corporate employers, but we wanted to explore ways in which they expressed themselves and made their own impact on their physical surroundings.

The specific way we approached these questions was to excavate their backyards. While these areas were owned by the corporation, they were used by the workers. By examining these spaces archaeologically we were able to learn how people used the yards over time. This was just a start, however. Through interdisciplinary analysis we could investigate these yards as microenvironments; their use over time, what other plants and animals lived there

Backyard Archaeology

Excavating a backyard may not seem to be a fruitful approach to learning about people's lives, but there are several reasons we were as interested in the backyards as in the houses. For one thing, we knew exactly where the houses were because we had detailed historical maps, and we knew what they looked like from existing plans, a restored sister block of buildings, and photographs and drawings. We knew much less about the physical appearance of the backyards.

Yet finding out what the backyards looked like was only one detail in which we were interested. There is a lot to be learned from excavating a yard, because that is where much of the day-to-day living debris ends up. A large part of backyard archaeology consists of looking at people's garbage. What people throw away, how they dispose of it, and where they put it tell us something about what they care about and what their attitudes are toward their living spaces. Specific questions to be investigated were how well-cared for the yards were, whether they had been landscaped or maintained by the Boott corporation, and what kinds of activities might have taken place there.

The archaeologists excavated thousands of artifacts, conducted chemical analyses on the soil, extracted pollen and phytoliths, and spent several years researching written records—all to learn everything they could about the workers who inhabited the Boott Mills boardinghouses. The rest of this book is devoted to specific topics on which information was gathered during the Lowell investigations. Taken together, these topics reflect the fabric of everyday life in Lowell as experienced by at least some of the Boott Mills' textile workers.

Lowell's Urban Landscape

A Landscape Changed

Before the mill corporations moved in, the site where Lowell would be built was a farming community known as East Chelmsford. There were farmhouses, fields, and pastures along the shores of the Concord and Merrimack Rivers, in addition to a number of milling operations taking advantage of the water power to be had from the rivers. This landscape would be dramatically altered in order to make the setting suitable for large-scale textile manufacturing. Since much of the land was part of the flood plain for the two rivers and therefore wet and unstable, large quantities of earth had to be brought in to level the ground and make it solid enough to support large buildings. Deep features such as privy shafts or foundations were not dug into glacial subsoil, as would normally be the case, but into soil filled with artifacts from even older sites, reduced to landfill.

After filling in the land, canals had to be built, in some cases through the fill. These canals brought water inland from the rivers to the mill machinery through the use of water wheels. In addition to all this filling and earthmoving, the mills themselves and the buildings that would house the workers had to be constructed.

Finally, landscaping that would make people feel comfortable and more at home had to be completed. Trees and grass had to be planted, fences put up, and streets and paths laid out. The result of this work was a new city that completely transformed the rural landscape of East Chelmsford.

The Planned City

The City of Lowell was the result of careful planning. The appearance of the buildings and of the landscapes gives us an idea of the impression the planners of Lowell intended to convey to the various city residents. The sources for this information are written records, paintings, drawings, photographs, archaeological excavations, and examinations of existing buildings. From all this evidence it seems that, at least in the early years of operation, the mill owners tried to make Lowell look and feel well cared for and more like home than like a grim, impersonal city. One of the early millworkers of Lowell, Lucy Larcom, described the way "long stretches of open land between the corporation buildings and the street made the town seem country-like." Indeed, it was to the corporations' benefit to make the city attractive since the mill owners needed to bring people there to work. A closer look at the Kirk Street agents' house and the boardinghouses will illustrate some of the city's prominent features.

Kirk Street Agents' House

The Kirk Street agents' house was a duplex built in 1845 to house the highest-level managers of two textile mills, the Boott Mills and the

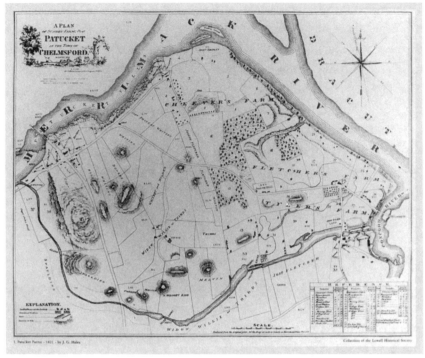

12. *Hale's 1822 map of "Patucket Farms in the town of Chelmsford," which was chosen by the Boston Associates for the site of Lowell.*

Massachusetts Mills. The corporations wanted to convey a sense of authority through the design of this structure, and therefore it was quite formal.

Everything about the Kirk Street agents' house spoke of power. It was close to the boardinghouses but raised above the other structures and above the street on an artificial terrace held in place by impressive, cut-granite blocks. It was also cut off from the boardinghouses by an imposing wrought-iron fence that enclosed its entire yard. The rear yard allotted to the household of each agent was initially nearly as large as the yard space to the rear of one of the boardinghouse units, although the agent's family shared the yard with no one. Even the building materials were of high quality: pressed brick with brown-

13. Lowell in 1825 looking north across the Merrimack River.

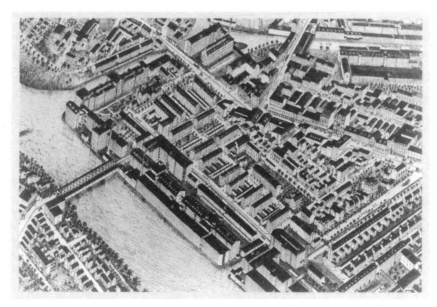

14. Bird's-eye view of Lowell, 1876.

15. Kirk Street agents' house as it appeared in 1988.

stone trim, dressed granite at the foundation level, and wood-paneled double doors. The front and side yards, which were visible from the street, were planted and maintained with a lawn, a fact supported by the thick layers of rich soil encountered by the archaeologists.

The Boardinghouses

The rows of boardinghouses that were built nearby between 1835 and 1839 conveyed a different message. Although they too were meant to be inviting the most striking aspect of these structures, perhaps, was their orderliness and symmetry. Eight identical blocks of boarding-houses were originally constructed for the Boott Mills workers. Each block contained four boardinghouses flanked at either end by two ten-ements consisting of apartments for skilled workers, supervisory personnel, and their families. The building materials were plainer and cheaper than those used in the Kirk Street agents' house, and there were no formal front or side yards to suggest a life of leisure. These were neat, ordered townhouses designed for efficiency rather than comfort. The buildings were well maintained on the outside. They were whitewashed every year, and the corporations took pains to enforce standards of cleanliness: there are many letters on file reprimanding boarders for messy yards.

The Backyard Story

The backyards of the Kirk Street agents' house and the boarding-houses also told very different stories about how people in Lowell actually lived their lives. It made sense that the profit-minded corporation owners would want to idealize their manufacturing center, not only to attract workers but also to stave off criticism from politicians and farmers who campaigned against what they saw as the evils of industrialization. Think of the great lengths to which modern corporations go to convince potential customers that they are not insensitive profiteers but are ecologically responsible, caring people trying to improve our lives.

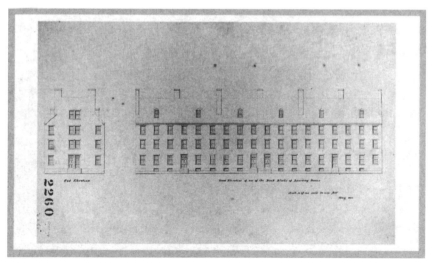

16. Front and end elevations of one of the Boott Blocks of boarding houses, 1836. (Locks and Canals Collection. Courtesy Lowell Historical Society and University of Massachusetts, Lowell, Center for Lowell History.)

Kirk Street Agents' House

Even the formal and well-maintained Kirk Street agents' house had a secret life, hidden in the backyard well away from the public's eye. Archaeological excavations showed that this was a working yard where all kinds of activities occurred.

The chemistry of the soil was examined, and high levels of phosphates and calcium were found. This was interpreted as evidence that garbage was allowed to decay there, a finding that was supported by the many animal bones that were also found in the yard. These were mostly bones from cuts of meat, but some were waste parts such as head and feet, suggesting that some slaughtering or butchering went on behind the scenes. There were also no layers of rich landscaping soil in the backyard, just lots of domestic trash. This was apparently an open yard used for washing, food processing, and garbage disposal. Of course, it was probably servants, not the agents' families, who worked in the yard. The families might have rarely entered the backyard since they had an indoor bathroom.

One of the more interesting things we learned about the Kirk Street agents' house backyard came from pollen and phytolith analyses, which suggested that weeds were gradually replaced by grasses. This meant that the yard became more ornamental over time, for as any gardener knows, you have to make a deliberate effort to get rid of weeds and grow grass instead. By the end of the time that mill agents lived in the house, the backyard was much more like a modern backyard—a place for playing and relaxation rather than for work. This was not true of the boarding-house backyards.

Back to the Boardinghouses

Each boardinghouse had an enclosed backyard that seemed too small for recreational activities but was used as a working yard. These yards were approximately 25 ft. x 25 ft. in size. Our excavations revealed the typical layout of these yards. Connected to the back of the house was a bulkhead entry to the basement and a small back room containing part of a well that was shared with the adjoining boardinghouse. At

17. Excavated rear yard of Boardinghouse Unit #48, Tenement.

the rear of the yard was a woodshed with a stone-lined privy pit in it.

The yards of the boardinghouses contained all kinds of trash and garbage. Archaeological evidence suggested that conditions in the boardinghouse backyards deteriorated over time. Bones and other refuse seem to have been thrown in pits or within the cellar in the early years of occupation, thus concealing them from view. Later on they seem to have been strewn randomly across the yard with little regard for appearances. This 1889 letter from the management to a boardinghouse tenant gives an idea of what many of the yards might have looked like in later years:

> Complaint is made that your family throws swill teagrounds etc. into the cesspool in your backyard and the same has clogged the drain and will have to be cleaned out which our Mr. Crawford will attend to, but you must stop throwing such stuff into the drain and not have it [happen] again, and use your swill bucket for such things. [A]lso you had a dead cat in your ash barrel last Friday which had lain so long that it was maggatey. You must be

18. Plan of excavated rear yaard of Boardinghouse Unit #45.

more cleanly, and not have so much litter about your premises, as it will breed disease and can't be allowed.

The landscaping evidence mirrored this trend toward laxness. For the early years of the Boott's history there were relatively high and stable levels of grass pollen, which suggested that the yards were well maintained. In later years the pollen record became dominated by weeds. Many seeds from the common New England weed nightshade were also found. This weed is a climber and probably clustered along the fences at the edges of the yards. The center of the yards seemed to have been left to dust and mud, although the discovery of wooden planks suggested that they may have been covered.

Lest we paint a more squalid picture of the urban landscape than really existed, we should point out that people in the boardinghouse did make some efforts to beautify their backyards. We found planting holes that probably housed small trees or shrubs. One hole had elderberry pollen and seeds in it, identifying it as the location of an elderberry bush. (Elderberries were used to make a popular cider.) We also found grape pollen and seeds in various parts of the yard, along with a series of holes for posts that might have supported a grape arbor. Even though both these plants were potentially useful as food, they must also have softened the otherwise harsh, utilitarian appearance of the yards.

In any case, the way the backyards of the Kirk Street agents' house and the boardinghouses were used was not at all unusual for the time. Outside spaces were much more utilitarian in the 1800s than they are today. What we discovered about the Lowell backyards through archaeological investigations is interesting for several other reasons. For one thing, the yards at the Kirk Street agents' house showed the transition from utilitarian to decorative, starting with a formal front and side yard combined with a working backyard, and ending with no outdoor working space at all. It is interesting to observe that the boardinghouses demonstrated the exact opposite trend, moving from a well-maintained, though probably working, yard to a weedy, trash-strewn city lot.

What both yards show best, though, is the reality of the urban landscape—a landscape lived in and used by people despite the best efforts of the corporations to portray it as a neat, controlled environment.

Living Conditions of
Boott Mills Workers

As we have seen, historical archaeologists pursue many lines of evidence in their attempts to go beyond written and oral statements that glorify the past and ignore or gloss over its variety, complexity, and humble or ignoble characteristics. Because the methods we use can reveal conditions as people in the past truly experienced them, we are able to examine the quality of life at its most intimate. The archaeological record provides clues about how people used the spaces available to them in the boardinghouses for acceptable as well as illicit activities; it tells of cleanliness and sanitation, or the lack thereof; and it yields details about the properties of water, soil, and other elements of the immediate environment that affected everyday life. Even the smallest of archaeological finds, something as plain and simple as a sherd from a broken flowerpot, can indicate actions people took to improve or embellish themselves and their surroundings.

Life in an Urban Boardinghouse

We know the basic layout of the boardinghouses by looking at old floor plans and by examining the one remaining structure in Lowell as well as similar buildings that survive in other communities. There was a dining room, a sitting room, a washing and storage area, and rooms for the boardinghouse keeper on the first floor. The second and third floors contained bedrooms shared by boarders and heated

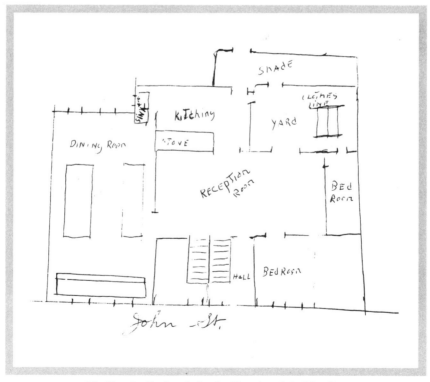

19. Blanche Graham's sketch of interior of the John Street boardinghouse she lived in as a child.

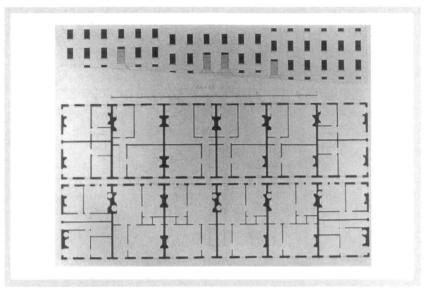

20. Floor plans and elevations for Boott Mills boardinghouses, 1836.
(Proprietors of Locks and Canals Collection. Courtesy of University of Massachusetts,
Lowell Special Collections.)

by fireplaces. Unlike the Kirk Street agents' house, there were no modern conveniences. Throughout the 1800s residents had to use an outdoor privy in the shed at the back of the yard. There was no sense of privacy in the boardinghouses either. According to an early resident, as many as six people had to share a room measuring 14 ft. x 16 ft., "with all the trunks, and boxes necessary to their convenience." Even though privacy was not commonplace in the 1800s under any circumstances, before coming to Lowell, mill workers probably had not been accustomed to sharing their space with strangers.

A more intimate view of the boardinghouses is offered by the memories of Blanche Graham. She lived in the boardinghouse as a child with her parents who worked in the mills during the early years of the twentieth century. She remembers entering the building into a long hallway that led into a reception room with wooden tables and chairs where men sat and talked and played cards. She remembers the dining room with three long wooden tables and the kitchen with a sink and a black stove along one wall. Her description of her youth reveals a stark existence: "[There] wasn't much furniture, cause them days they didn't have much furniture. . . . Mattress was like straw or some darn thing . . . or maybe feathers . . . and wooden chairs, everything was wood . . . there was no fanciness. Maybe a plain wooden bureau with a few drawers to put your clothes in and a mirror to stick up on the wall. That was the furniture."

As Blanche remembers, the lighting was kerosene and there was just one water closet containing a toilet and a sink with cold running water. This one bathroom was for the entire house. There were chamber pots in everyone's bedroom. This was, however, an improvement on the outdoor privy that was used by boardinghouse residents during the 1800s.

Sanitation

Privies were not a very pleasant solution for the problem of human waste. With the number of people using them at the boardinghouses, they would have required fairly frequent cleaning to keep them from becoming offensive. In Lowell this task was accomplished through what was called the "night-cart" system. Farmers from outlying areas were given licenses to clean privies and cart off the city's sewerage and rubbish during the evening (hence, "night-workers"). This system proved unsatisfactory as problems with leaking night-carts and the farmers' demands for higher wages exceeded the benefits of maintaining the privies.

By 1890 the Board of Health of the City of Lowell ordered that all privies be abandoned and replaced by water closets hooked up to sewer lines. Archaeological investigations showed that the corporations were slow to comply with the law. Over seven hundred machine-made bottle fragments were excavated from two privies in the boardinghouse backyards. Because the process for making this kind of bottle was not put into use until 1910, we know that the privies were not abandoned and filled in until at least 1910, twenty years after the city demanded that it be done.

Because of the privies, drinking water was unsanitary for the boardinghouse residents. Most water was obtained from wells in the backyard or from the canals. The wells were easily subject to contamination because they were shallow and were placed too close to the privies—a look at the layout of the backyards confirms this. The canals were no cleaner. Stepped tower privies were used in all the mills along the canals, and the human waste was released directly into the water. The city began to provide piped water as early as the 1870s, but many boardinghouses continued to rely on their primitive sources into the 1890s.

One unpleasant side effect of these unsanitary conditions was that the boardinghouse residents had to put up with rats. Blanche Graham remembered rats at her boardinghouse, and we found plenty of evidence of them in the archaeological record. Not only did we find rat bones, but we also found evidence of their eating habits. Many of the animal bones and plant remains found in the boardinghouse backyard had rodent gnaw marks on them. This was in stark contrast to the evidence from the Kirk Street agents' house, where no rat bones were found and only one piece of bone showed signs of having been gnawed. The rats probably preferred the boardinghouse not only because of its more unsanitary conditions, but also because food was stored in bulk in the basement. The presence of rats in one place and their absence in the other pointed to a fundamental difference in the quality of life experienced by these two groups of people.

Hygiene

It did not surprise any of us to learn that working in the mills was a very dirty business. The various processes involved in making cloth released clouds of lint that stuck to bodies covered with sweat and machine grease. Washing facilities at the boardinghouses were not equal to the task of keeping the residents clean. We would probably consider the

21. Lewis Hine photograph of washday in a Homestead, Pennsylvania, boardinghouse backlot. (Reproduced from Byington, 1910.)

workers' personal hygiene inadequate by today's standards.

Before we make any judgments about the cleanliness of boardinghouse residents, however, we have to understand the facilities with which they had to live. There was no running water as we know it today in the boardinghouses. As we have already mentioned, water was brought in from a well in the backyard. A lead pipe found in one of the wells may have carried water to a cistern in the basement or to the kitchen. Just when water hook-ups were installed is unclear, however. Even in the early twentieth century bathing facilities were nonexistent.

The hardships of doing laundry contributed additional problems to workers trying to keep clean. Clothing was scrubbed in a tub of water and hung on a line to dry, a procedure that took a considerable amount of time. One of the privileges of boarding was that your bed linens were washed for you by the boardinghouse keeper. Personal clothing was not included, however, and would have been either sent out to be laundered for a price or washed during precious leisure time.

Several artifacts related to personal grooming were found in the boardinghouse excavations. We recovered two kinds of combs that were used in grooming. One was the regular straight comb used to get tangles out, but the other was a fine toothed comb. Fine-toothed combs were used in the 1800s to comb dirt and lice out of the hair. Another piece of evidence for remedial grooming came in the form of glass cosmetic and cologne containers, several of which were excavated from the backyards. These small luxuries were probably prized possessions that aided personal hygiene. They would have helped to disguise the odors and irregularities of complexion that might result from infrequent bathing.

Health

Our current understanding of germs as the agents of disease was not fully accepted until the very end of the 1800s. For most of the nineteenth century people believed that disease was carried in clouds of poisonous gases (miasmas) emitted by decaying waste. The only defense against disease borne by these threatening vapors was plenty of sunlight, ventilation, and dryness, all of which the corporations recommended but did not provide. And, as we have seen, the very sources of these "miasmas"—the accumulated refuse in the back-yards, the uncapped privy vaults, and the contaminated wells—were not attended to. Even considering the disease theory of the day, workers did not live in very healthful conditions, and the real culprits—including viruses and bacteria that spread through human contact and in contaminated drinking water—were allowed to run rampant.

Sickness was a frightening reality of life in Lowell in the 1800s and early 1900s. Diseases that are seldom a threat to Americans today could kill hundreds of people in the prime of life a hundred years ago. A case in point is the influenza epidemic of 1918, which spread throughout the world. This disease, called Spanish Influenza, was a particularly virulent strain of the flu virus that circulates throughout the population every year. We all know the aches and chills and congestion associated with the flu, but the Spanish strain attacked the lungs and brought on pneumonia, most frequently in young people between the ages of

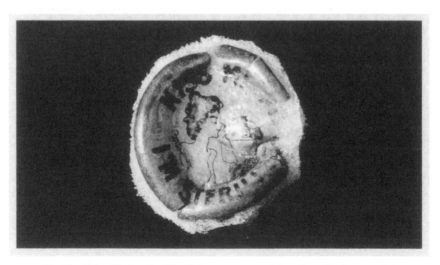

22. The "Kiss Me I'm Sterilized" button recovered from boardinghouse privy.

twenty one and twenty nine. Lowell was hit by the flu epidemic in the fall of 1918, and during the week of October 6–12, 141 influenza-related deaths were reported.

That this outbreak was a part of the Lowell workers' consciousness was made apparent by a particularly fascinating artifact excavated from the fill of a privy vault. It was a plastic pin-back button resembling a campaign button. It depicted a man and a woman kissing and surrounded by the words, "KISS ME [illegible] I'M STERILIZED." The figures were rendered with simple lines to create a cartoonish effect, with costumes and hairstyles suggesting a date of the early 1900s. What was most curious was an object protruding from the woman's right shoulder that looked like a hypodermic needle. It seemed that this button was meant to advertise the fact that the wearer had been vaccinated against a disease (probably the Spanish Influenza) and was safe for kissing!

The Personal Touch

Few Americans today would be comfortable living with the conditions of sanitation, hygiene, and health that prevailed in the boardinghouses of Lowell in the 1800s. Although the domestic technology for improving conditions was not available to all citizens until the early twentieth century, the middle-class residents of the Kirk Street agents' house enjoyed a much higher standard of living during the mid-nineteenth century. The house was equipped with indoor plumbing, including running water in the kitchen and water closets for the residents. Even when the technology for indoor plumbing became available, the corporations seemed to have been reluctant to spend money on improvements to the boardinghouses. As a result, the boarders lived in an atmosphere that was not only unpleasant, but, in some cases, unhealthy.

In the face of this rather harsh environment people did what they could to make the place feel like home and to express their individuality. Some keepers, who furnished their houses with an eye to economy, seemed to have lavished attention on the parlor where the residents convened and guests were received. One visitor to a Lowell boardinghouse in 1886 remarked on how "handsomely-furnished" the parlor was. The room was equipped with a carpet, wallpaper, curtains, framed prints on the walls, upholstered chairs, a table with knickknacks, and a piano. (This is certainly more welcoming than the sparsely furnished card room of Blanche Graham's memory!)

Other attempts at beautification were found in the archaeological record. We have already mentioned the elderberries and grapes planted in the backyards; we also found many fragments of plant pots, suggesting that the keeper and the boarders raised plants somewhere in or around the boardinghouse. We do not know whether these pots were used to grow herbs for use in the kitchen or to grow flowers.

Life in the boardinghouses may have been cramped and lacking in privacy, but no doubt many residents found that the benefits of communal living outweighed its shortcomings. Nevertheless the archaeological evidence for deteriorating conditions at the boardinghouses is unmistakable. We would be wrong, however, to project our own standards of cleanliness and hygiene onto the past without attempting to comprehend the experiences of nineteenth-century workers and their notions of what was appropriate and acceptable. Archaeology offers us raw data, the "naked truth" that needs to be interpreted within the cultural and historical context not of our own times but of the people whom we seek to learn more about through our work. Close examination of artifacts that reflect positive and constructive actions by boardinghouse residents to take charge of some parts of their lives teaches us that workers who resided here were not all hapless victims of industrialization but people who were proud of their work, proud of their appearance, and, indeed, proud of themselves.

Mealtimes at the Boott

Food must have had special meaning for Boott Cotton Mills textile workers as meals provided precious moments away from the stressful pace and long hours of work. Indeed, food is an integral part of everyone's life, and historical archaeologists do more than just study which foods people ate in the past. They are also interested in the way food was produced, the manner in which it was prepared, and even how food remains were discarded. Historical archaeology is well suited to studying all dimensions of diet—a perspective that we call "foodways". We can dig up the remains of meals in the form of animal bones and plant seeds and the fragments of the dishes and cutlery with which the food was served. From these material remains, as well as information from documents, memories, and photographs, we can gain an understanding of how the workers of the Boott spent their mealtimes.

Working-Class Meals

Mealtimes at the boardinghouses were a very different kind of experience from the family meals most of us enjoy today. For the price of a room, a boarder was also given three meals a day. The meals were

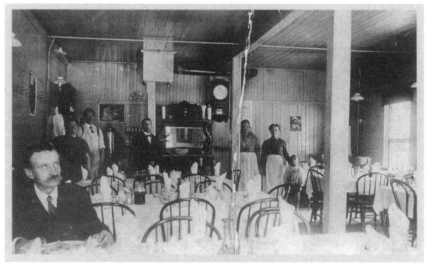

*23. The dining room at Croteau's boardinghouse, ca. 1908.
(Courtesy of Lowell National Park.)*

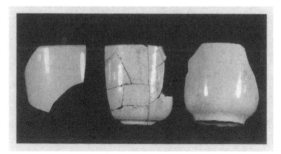

*24. Plain whiteware cup fragments recovered from
boardinghouse yard.*

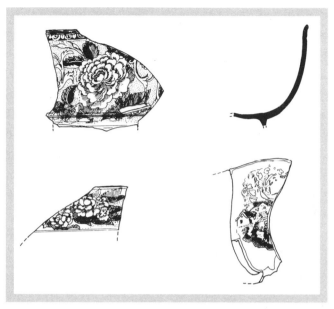

25. Pearlware with cobalt blue transfer printing and purple lustre glaze. The print is a floral design manufactured between 1795 and 1840 in England. Cup fragments recovered from yard of the Kirk Street agent's house.

served in the dining room, where all boarders would come together to eat. Rows of tables were set for everyone, and the food was brought in on large platters or in bowls from which the diners served themselves.

The Table

A total of 7,183 ceramic fragments, accounting for a minimum of 305 individual dishes, were excavated from the backyards of Boott units #45, the boardinghouse, and #48, the tenement. Of these dishes, almost 75 percent were made of an inexpensive and utilitarian material called whiteware. More than a third of these dishes were completely undecorated. Apparently the boardinghouse table was set mostly with plain white dishes.

The impression of stark table settings was reinforced by other aspects of the ceramic analysis. Of the ceramic fragments that were decorated, none of the patterns matched any other except in color, suggesting that little effort was made to obtain matched sets. Apparently, the motivating force behind tableware choice was cost.

The inexpensive, mismatched dinnerware bespoke a quiet humility but mealtimes were probably lively, filled with talk of work, talk of family, and talk of leisure time. In contrast, the table at the agents' house was set with matching plates, saucers, and serving platters, colorful and attractive dishes with transfer-printed scenes of exotic ruins and foreign locales. Fine glassware and silverplate must have been carefully laid out by servants. Here, the family and its guests were waited on and served.

The kinds of ceramic vessels in the collection can also tell us something about how the meals were served. At the boardinghouse there were mostly plates, large platters, and bowls, suggesting the communal nature of the food service. There were also very few specialized forms such as vegetable dishes, bread plates, or salad plates. Boardinghouse residents were apparently provided with only the basics for food service and consumption. Complete meals were served to individuals on a single plate with few or no accessories, reducing the number of dishes the boardinghouse keeper had to purchase, carry, wash, and replace, and rendering meals straightforward and practical.

Things were only slightly better for the families living in the tenements. Here one difference was the presence of tea services. Although the ceramics were not fancy, they did evoke images of family life that might not have been common in the boardinghouses. To share tea with the family or others was a form of entertainment not open to many of the mill workers.

Meal Choice

The food served was the choice of the boardinghouse keeper and not the individual residents. It was probably also chosen with economy in mind because the keeper was trying to make a decent living. Written records show that keepers bought grains, flour, and vegetables in bulk and stored them in the basement. There are no recorded complaints about the food, although it seems that to the tenants quantity was as important as quality. Blanche Graham described boardinghouse meals this way: "In the mornin' you had bacon and eggs and all that stuff. It was good food, oh yeah. If you felt like toast, French toast, or oatmeal, then she had it. At dinnertime she'd have maybe a big corn beef and cabbage dinner . . . . At supper, well ya had a light supper. She'd warm it up and give it to you."

An analysis of the kinds of bones found during the excavations contributes some insights about the meat portion of the meal. Even though the numbers are small, the food bones identified show that there was some variety in the boarders' meals. Cow, pig, sheep, goat, and chicken bones were found, but it seems that beef dominated their diet.

The kind of meat eaten is not the only information that the bones have to tell. The zooarchaeologist also looked at marks on the bones to determine how the meat was butchered and what cuts of meat were purchased by the boardinghouse keeper and prepared for the boarders. A total of ninety-five bones had butchery marks on them, the majority of which were shears or saw marks. These are primary butchery marks, those resulting from the initial division of the carcass. Many of these bones could be identified according to what cut of meat they were, an important criterion in determining standard of living. The results were somewhat surprising in that there was much more variety than expected. Apparently, the boardinghouse residents were served not only cost-efficient leg of mutton, but also more expensive cuts such as beef short loin and sirloin.

Meat was not the only component of the boarders' diet, but it is the most identifiable type of food archaeologically. Another source of information about food is plant remains, both macroscopic (seeds) and microscopic (pollen). Seeds found in the privy (and therefore probably consumed by the boardinghouse residents) included strawberry, blueberry, and blackberry. Other areas of the yards contained seeds of peach and elderberry. Both pollen and seeds of grape were found, indicating that grapes may not have been just eaten, but also grown in the boardinghouse backyards. It is certain from this evidence that fruits constituted part of the boardinghouse residents' diet, whether eaten fresh, as pie filling, or as preserves.

A Telling Comparison

One way to understand what mealtimes were like in the boardinghouses is to explore how they might have differed from a family meal served at the home of the wealthier mill agents. The excavations behind the agent's house on neighboring Kirk Street provided this comparative information. We could probably assume that mealtimes at the Kirk Street agents' house and at the boardinghouses must have been very different experiences. The former was likely a small family gathering with servants in attendance, while the latter was a boisterous communal affair that brought together people who shared a living space and working experience. Through archaeological excavations, however, we were able to put our finger on precisely how these differences might be expressed in the physical aspects of mealtimes.

It was with some surprise that we discovered that it was not in the food itself, but rather in the way it was served, that the managers were distinguished from the workers in nineteenth-century Lowell. Of the bones left to rot in the backyard of the agents' house, more than half of those that could be identified were cow bones. Beef was apparently the preferred meat, although pork, lamb, fish, turkey, and chicken bones were also found. The cuts of these meats were also identified, and it was surprising to note that inexpensive cuts were much more usual than expensive ones. We had expected that, because company agents made more money than the mill workers, they could afford more expensive cuts of meat. The *kind* of food served, then, was apparently not particularly lavish or extravagant, but the *way* it was served might have been.

The tableware we excavated from the Kirk Street agents' house backyard belied the rather commonplace selection of meats. We found large sets of fancy English china decorated with floral motifs, travel and landscape scenes, and geometric patterns in colors of brown, blue, green, black, purple, and red. We also found evidence of fine glassware and glass globes from gaslights, which were a new innovation. Many of the dishes were large bowls or platters from which food was probably served by the domestic help. While the agents and their families ate rather plain meals off sumptuous china, the boardinghouse residents generally ate the same plain meals served on starkly plain white china or occasionally on decorated tableware.

Leisure Time at the Boott

We have devoted much of our discussion to those aspects of workers' lives that were controlled by the company. Now we can turn our attention to what the workers did with some of the little time they had left to themselves. Between working in the mills and eating meals with fellow workers, boardinghouse residents had very little leisure time. We know from looking at the written record that this was particularly true of the early years of Lowell when the work force was dominated by young women from the New England countryside. In order to reassure the families of these young women that their morality was being looked after, the corporations adopted a paternal role and tried to control even the leisure time of the work force. Rules and regulations were established, including the requirements that workers live in company-run boardinghouses (which would be locked at 10:00 P.M.), attend Sunday church services, and not drink alcohol. Work hours were long, usually from Monday through Saturday, leaving workers with only a few hours in the evenings and on Sundays to do as they pleased.

After 1840, the composition of the work force shifted as the New England farmgirls abandoned the mills and were replaced by immigrant labor. The "moral" control exercised by the corporations seemed to wane at this time. Workers were no longer required to live in company-run boardinghouses, and there were no recorded church requirements or bans on alcohol. The published regulations focused more on the responsibilities of the keepers, most of which were related to insuring an income for the corporations. Leisure time was still as scarce as it was before 1840, but it seemed that what workers did with it was less prescribed by the corporations. It is this period after 1840 that we investigated archaeologically.

The backyard of the boardinghouse was one of the places where workers might have spent some of their leisure hours, particularly in the short evenings between meals and bedtime when it would have been difficult to go anywhere far from home. It is easy to imagine people gathering in the backyard on a warm summer evening, playing cards, mulling over the events of the day, and sharing opinions or gossip with a housemate or neighbor. While the boardinghouse residents socialized, some indulged in a drink or a smoke, evidence of which we found during the archaeological investigations. There were many pipes and pieces of broken bottles buried in the backyards. These unprepossessing artifacts sparked our interest and led us to some very interesting conclusions about how these activities were incorporated into the everyday lives of textile workers.

Cigars and Cutties

Smoking today is rapidly declining in popularity in the United States as the public learns more and more about the risks it poses to health and longevity. Smoking had few of these negative connotations in the 1800s. What you smoked and where you smoked, however, were very

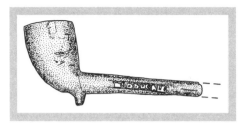

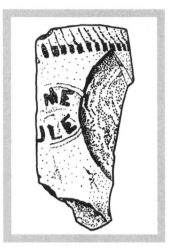

26. Clay pipe with McDougall stamped on stem and T. (TD) on bowl. Made by McDougall & Co., Glasgow, Scotland.

27. Pipe bowl embossed with "Home Rule" slogan dating to the 1880s.

much tied up with who you were and to what social class you belonged. As long as you smoked in a manner suited to your station in life, smoking was pretty well accepted.

Cigarettes did not become widely available until the end of the nineteenth century. Before that, middle- and upper-class men tended to smoke cigars because they were expensive and to smoke long pipes because the highly fragile stems implied the ability to smoke in a leisurely manner. The length of a pipe was a matter of some importance. The longer the shaft, the cooler the smoke would be by the time it reached the mouth. Yet a long pipe required special attention. The smoker had to hold the pipe in one hand, and sometimes even had to be seated to control it properly. Only a man of considerable leisure would have the time to smoke a long pipe. Within the middle and upper classes, smoking was mostly limited to men since women who smoked risked being considered "loose."

Among the working classes, clay pipes were favored. These were much less expensive than cigars and could be broken to any desired length. Shorter pipes, called "cutties," were preferable to a working person because they could be gripped by the teeth and did not require a free hand. This allowed the smoker to partake while on the

28. Nineteenth-century illustrations showing woman seated and smoking a pipe.

29. Three one-pint liquor bottles recovered from the boardinghouse backyard.

job, though a textile worker would never have been allowed to smoke at work because of the danger of fire. Another difference in working-class smoking behavior was that women were not barred from the activity.

It was with interest and an eye to these known class distinctions that we examined the nearly five hundred white clay pipe fragments that were excavated from the boardinghouse backyards. Some of the pipes had marks on them that indicated their manufacturer. Most of these were marked "T.D.," the name of a very inexpensive kind of pipe that cost only a few cents. Some of the markings suggested political affiliations. "HOME RULE," which referred to the Irish fight for independence from the British, appeared on several pipes, and one pipe even bore the name of Wolf Tone, an Irish political martyr. These are clear indications of working-class and ethnic identity being expressed through smoking paraphernalia.

Another interesting finding was the archaeological evidence of

modifications to the pipes. It was clear that many of the pipes had
been deliberately broken to make them shorter because almost none
of the identifiable factory-made mouthpieces had any tooth marks on
them. In contrast, many of the stem fragments had tooth marks or
showed marks of having been modified by whittling or grinding, for
example. One stem fragment showed signs of having been deeply
scored with a knife and then snapped at that point. It was apparent
that short pipes were more useful to the working-class boardinghouse
residents, and that if the pipes they bought were not short enough,
they could easily be made so.

Alcohol

Within the middle class in the mid- to late-1800s, there was a strong
temperance or anti-alcohol movement headed by social reformers,
which ultimately led to the legal prohibition of alcohol during the
1920s. These views were not held by everybody, but the middle-class

30. Soda bottles of P. Kelley & Co., manufactured in Lowell.

31. Cache of liquor bottles found outside a boardinghouse privy.

opponents were in positions of power, which enabled them to influence public opinion and successfully portray alcohol consumption as a vice that was responsible for crime, insanity, and poverty.

Apparently the Lowell corporations concurred with the reformers. While company regulations did not explicitly state a prohibition on alcohol, letters from the company to boardinghouse keepers made it clear that excessive drunkenness was a serious offense. One letter from 1899 said, "We are informed that Annie Driscoll . . . has been drunk at your house all this week—You probably know that this is contrary to your order from agt. and that all cases of drunkenness must be reported to the counting room. You will at once dismiss Driscoll from your house."

This policy was instituted primarily for the good of the corporation. Drunken employees would slow production, threaten profits, and give a bad public impression. Moreover, inebriated workers might injure themselves, causing additional problems and disruptions.

The archaeological evidence made it clear that boardinghouse residents imbibed alcohol despite company policy discouraging it. Thousands of glass fragments were excavated from the boardinghouse backyards. Among these were pieces of wine glasses, beer mugs, and at least seventy two individual alcohol bottles, including flasks for hard liquor as well as wine and beer bottles. These flasks and bottles probably represent just a small percentage of what was purchased by the residents over the course of the century, since bottles could be returned for a deposit and many probably were returned, for reasons of economy.

Two important observations can be made about the collection of alcohol vessels. For one thing, they seem to have been bought with economy in mind. Most of the liquor bottles were small, suggesting that workers could only afford small amounts at a time. They also contained locally made brands, which were less expensive than imported brands.

The second observation is that workers may have tried to conceal the evidence of their drinking from prying eyes. The smallness of the bottles, while probably due to economic necessity, also allowed them to be easily hidden in pockets or bags. The bottles seem to have been discarded in out-of-the-way places, such as corners of buildings or fence lines, in the privies, and in what would have been crawlspaces beneath buildings. The strongest evidence of secrecy was a "cache" of whole bottles found in the wood shed at the back of the boardinghouse yard near the privy. The fact that the bottles remained largely intact suggested that they were carefully placed somewhere protected, such as under a step, a platform, or even the woodshed floor. Perhaps workers drank in the woodshed where neither keepers nor agents could see them and then hid the bottles, either empty or full.

Such indications that the workers drank in secret does not mean, however, that they all thought of their behavior as illicit. When we look at the evidence for alcohol use in the boardinghouse backyards, it is important to keep in mind that most of the workers living there in the late 1800s were immigrants who may not have shared the

American middle-class view of alcohol. These people came from cultures that may have accepted alcohol rather than considering it a vice. It was only when they came to this country that what they considered normal behavior was transformed into something that had to be hidden. Had they been able to afford their own homes, perhaps they would not have been as subject to the corporations' middle-class morality and would not have been forced into clandestine behavior.

Postscript

Smoking and drinking were just two leisure activities in which mill workers engaged, and there were probably many individuals who did neither. The nature of archaeological investigation, however, is that we can examine only *tangible* remains of people's activities. We cannot know through archaeology how much time people spent talking, sewing, reading, singing, or playing, although oral testimony indicates that such activities were common. As it happens, smoking and drinking leave behind plentiful artifactual evidence, and thus become the focus of our investigation of leisure behavior.

Clothing and Personal Adornment

Clothing and personal ornaments were some of the very few items that workers purchased for themselves, and for this reason they must have had personal significance. By looking at the artifacts of clothing and personal adornment, archaeologists can learn something about how the workers who lived in the Lowell boardinghouses chose to express themselves.

Archaeology, though not without its limitations, has advantages over written history for this kind of investigation. For one thing, contemporary written sources tend to focus on high fashion as opposed to the kinds of clothes working-class people might have worn. Just think about today's Vogue magazine, or the fashion pages of the New York Times. These hardly convey a sense of the kinds of clothes most people wear to work every day, or the blue jeans, t-shirts, and sneakers we don for leisure. Moreover, we are not so much interested in what most people wore as in what the particular people who lived in the boardinghouses wore. We can use the written record as a standard against which to compare the clothing habits of our subjects, but nothing in the written record tells us as much as the actual buttons, beads, and jewelry that these people bought and wore.

As we have already said, archaeology is not without its problems. Actual articles of clothing do not tend to survive buried in the ground. Cloth deteriorates fairly quickly unless it is preserved under very dry conditions. Even if we do find cloth, it is usually in the form of small fragments that are not very illuminating. What we frequently find are the accessories of clothing: beads, jewelry, buttons, and hair combs. Yet even these small items can tell us something about the people who used them.

32. Copper alloy brooch recovered from boardinghouse backyard.

Another drawback of archaeology is that the items we find are usually those that were discarded or lost. The most precious and valued personal possessions tend to be guarded by the owner. These are probably passed on from generation to generation as heirlooms, and are rarely found buried in someone's backyard. Despite these drawbacks, however, we did find some interesting objects and were able to identify their shared characteristics, which seemed to tell us something about the people who lived in the boardinghouses.

Jewelry and Beads

We excavated more than thirty items of jewelry, including beads, from the backyards of the two boardinghouses. Several pieces of jewelry were striking. There were two delicate round brooches with hinged pins that seemed to have contained photographic or painted miniatures at one time. Both pieces of jewelry were made of copper and had a similar design. One brooch with a braided border framed a piece of glass behind which the miniature was mounted. The other brooch, which was a round piece of metal onto which a photograph was mounted, had a swirling border that was suggestive of foliage.

Another handsome piece of jewelry that we excavated was a copper alloy and rhinestone pin that held nine clear glass stones in a

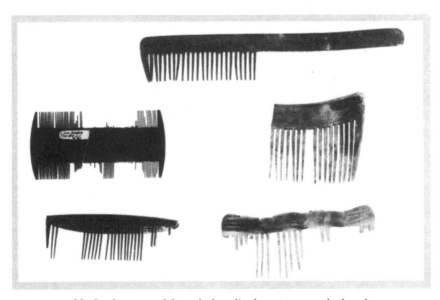

33. Combs recovered from the boardinghouse tenement backyards.

straight line. Had the stones been real, this would have been a very expensive and impressive piece of ornamentation. As costume jewelry, it probably was not very valuable, though it might have excited speculation among its owner's friends and acquaintances. In fact, one of the most interesting things about the jewelry that we found is that all of it was made from imitation materials that looked valuable, but were not. The female boardinghouse residents wanted to look fashionable while purchasing accessories that were within their means.

Hair Combs and Ornaments

Excavations in the backyards of the boardinghouses yielded more than forty hair combs and ornaments. Some of these were utilitarian combs used to get out tangles or remove dirt and lice, but many more were decorative combs that were used in women's hair. Women in the late 1800s wore their hair long and needed to keep it up and away from their faces. This was especially important for female textile workers, who risked injuries if their hair became entangled in the moving parts of looms, belts, or spinning machines. Combs and hairpins were placed at the back or top of the head according to the current style, and although fashions in hairstyles changed during the course of the century, short hair did not come into vogue until the 1920s.

Again, the overwhelming impression made by all of the combs and hair ornaments that we found was that they were made from imitation materials and must have been very inexpensive. Plastic was developed and marketed as early as 1870, and it was perfect for imitating genuine tortoise shell—a very expensive commodity. Most of the decorative hair combs and pins were made of plastic, some of which looked very much like tortoise shell. As was true with the jewelry, the hair decorations had to be both attractive and inexpensive. Because the boarders probably could not afford tortoise shell, they bought the next best thing: plastic.

Buttons and Studs

By far the most plentiful artifacts of clothing and personal adornment that we found were buttons and studs. Studs, like buttons, were used to fasten clothing. They have a short shaft attached to a knob or disk at either end and look sort of like miniature barbells. Each knob was put through a hole, one on each side of two pieces of clothing that were being fastened together. From the front, the stud would have looked just like a button with no holes. Studs were used by both men and women. From the middle of the 1700s, they were used by men to attach separate cuffs to their shirts. By the 1830s studs were used on the front of shirts as buttons are used today. Around 1860 men began to use separate collars because they were easier to wash, and studs were used to attach them to the shirts. Studs were also used on men's vests as well as on women's collars, cuffs, and shirtwaists, which were blouses or dresses that buttoned or "studded" down the front.

We excavated a total of 131 buttons and studs from the boardinghouse and tenement backyards. We found buttons and studs made of many materials, including metal, shell, plastic, wood, and glass, but more than three quarters of them were made of plain white porcelain. Most of the plain white buttons had two or four holes and looked very much like any white button one sees today. The difference was that the buttons we excavated in Lowell were made of porcelain, and the buttons you see today are usually made of shell or plastic. Shell buttons were available to consumers in the 1800s, but porcelain was much less expensive. They were advertised in the mail-order catalogs of the time as looking like shell, which suggests that people bought them as a cheaper substitute. Indeed, whereas shell buttons cost twenty cents per dozen in a Montgomery Ward mail-order catalog of 1895, porcelain buttons of the same size cost only ten cents for 144 buttons. We also found a number of buttons made of black glass and shaped into some very interesting and wonderful designs. One pair of buttons was faceted with a smiling man-in-the-moon silhouette fashioned along its edge. Another button had a swirling design of polished facets running down its center, reminiscent of galaxies in a clear night sky. Black glass was probably a substitute for the rare and expensive material "jet," which was made from a dense black coal. Jet ornaments became popular in the 1860s when Queen Victoria of England went into mourning for her husband, Albert. Once again, we see the women of the boardinghouses as having been interested in keeping up with fashions, but unable to pay the price.

The personal items we excavated from the boardinghouse backyards do not tell us the whole story of what people wore or how they adorned themselves, but they do allow us to make some interesting observations. Boardinghouse residents worked long hours and lived among strangers with very little space or time to themselves. On the plus side the mill workers received wages for their labors. For many, Lowell represented their first real economic freedom. Money could be used to purchase many things, including the types of personal items we recovered. Lowell was a town with many stores, and by the end of the century, numerous mail-order catalogs were available that allowed people to shop without leaving their homes. The boardinghouse residents apparently took advantage of these opportunities to stay abreast of changing fashions, even though their working-class wages forced them to make compromises in their purchases.

The Bigger Picture

Governed by the concept of corporate paternalism, the establishment of Lowell, Massachusetts, set in motion one of the largest and most innovative industrial experiments in America's history. We do not know whether the workers who toiled in the mills saw their labors as a contribution to a larger picture or whether they measured their lives week to week. Using the comprehensive approach of historical archaeology, we were able to retrieve part of the material world of the nineteenth-century mill workers. At the same time, we were able to chronicle the life-history of Lowell as an experiment. What we found was that by the late 1800s Lowell was an experiment whose luster had faded.

By the later years of the nineteenth century, boardinghouse yards that had once been well maintained were now weed-choked spaces strewn with trash. The presence of garbage in the yards attracted rats to the boardinghouses. Lead from paint chips and other sources

34. Stereopticon view, ca. 1889, showing unidentified workers standing outside the Boott housing in Amory Street. The Boott Mills complex is to the right; to the left, the end of the boardinghouse block can be seen.

made its way into yard soils and represented a health hazard for young children and adults alike. These observations, gleaned from the archaeological record, contribute to a portrait not unlike the images we have today of America's working poor. This picture was further refined by comparing our results from the boardinghouse with those from the tenement and the Kirk Street agents' house. At a time when the boardinghouses were starting to decay, the company was adding the latest in household innovations to the agent's house.

These differences extended to the yards that surrounded the buildings. The front and side yards of agents' house were tailored and neatly kept for public eyes. The backyard, however, was just as much a working yard as were the boardinghouse and tenement yards.

As living and working conditions continued to deteriorate, worker unrest grew. Workers' calls for improved wages, job security, and better working conditions went unheeded, leading to strikes and the formation of labor unions by the early decades of the twentieth century. This ushered in Lowell's final phase as a center for textile production. Eventually lower profits and competition from southern mills contributed to the closing of many of the mills. In some cases mill complexes and workers' housing were demolished.

In comparing what we found in the boardinghouse, tenement, and agents' house backyards, we were struck by the differences in the appearance of the yards and the manner in which meals were taken. Yet it may be wrong to make too much of these contrasts, as striking as they are. There is much that was shared by the many actors in Lowell's drama. What they shared was a new way of life, one that was distinctly urban in flavor. For many the city was exciting if not somewhat overwhelming. The pace of life contrasted sharply with rural living. There were stores, places to eat, and things to buy. And there were people, lots of people, from all over New England, and later from different parts of the world. This was city life.

From our perspective, life in the workers' housing may seem stark and underprivileged, but the archaeology can speak to us in other ways. Despite the seeming omnipresence of the corporation, workers made their own lives and took pride in their work, their personal appearance, and even in the yards of their corporation-owned homes. This is evident in the personal touches we detected in the backyards and in the wide array of items of personal adornment and grooming. Workers were certainly limited to some extent by their incomes, but even so, it seems clear that they were willing participants in the world of commerce. They expressed themselves in the jewelry, hair combs, and buttons they bought, and in the flowerpots with which they chose to decorate their homes. Some felt strongly enough about their own ethnic identities to communicate their pride in the pipes they smoked and perhaps even in the fruit vines they grew in their yards. Some people may have succumbed to the ill effects of alcohol, but most forged an indelible identity—a working-class culture that contributed in a powerful way to the changing fabric of American culture.

Sources and Further Reading

Introduction

Discussions of and histories of Lowell abound; some were written in the nineteenth century by people directly involved with the mills, and a number have been written in the twentieth century by traditional historians as well as by social, labor, and public historians.

Contemporary sources that justified and defended industrialization in Lowell include Nathan Appleton, *Introduction of the Power Loom and Origin of Lowell* (Lowell: B. H. Penhallow, 1858); Elisha Bartlett, *A Vindication of the Character and Condition of the Females Employed in the Lowell Mills Against the Charges in the* Boston Times *and the* Boston Quarterly Review (Lowell: Leonard Huntress, 1841); and Rev. Henry A. Miles, Lowell, *As It Was, and As It Is* (1846; Facsimile, New York: Arno Press, 1972).

Critics of the mills also had their say: Azer Ames, Jr., M.D., *Sex in Industry: A Plea for the Working Girl* (Boston: James R. Osgood & Co., 1875); James Cook Ayer, *Some of the Uses and Abuses in the Management of Our Manufacturing Corporations* (Lowell, 1863); Erastus B. Bigelow, *Remarks on the Depressed Condition of Manufactures in Massachusetts, with Suggestions as to Its Cause and Its Remedy* (Boston, 1858); and Female Labor Reform Association, *Factory Life as It Is, by an Operative* (1845; reprint, Lowell: Lowell Publishing Co., 1982).

Writings by the women who worked in the mills during Lowell's early decades include firsthand accounts, letters, autobiographies, and even short literary works such as those published in the "mill girls' own" periodical, *The Lowell Offering*. See Thomas Dublin, ed., *Farm & Factory: The Mill Experience and Women's Lives in New England, 1830-1860* (New York: Columbia University Press, 1982); Benita Eisler, ed., *The Lowell Offering: Writings by New England Mill Women, (1840–1845)* (New York: Harper Torchbooks, 1977); Lucy Larcom, *A New England Girlhood: Outlined from Memory* (1889; reprint, Boston: Northeastern University Press, 1986); Harriett H. Robinson, *Loom and Spindle, Or Life Among the Early Mill Girls* (Boston: Thomas V. Cromwell & Co., 1898).

Twentieth-century historians have examined many aspects of Lowell's industrial past, often revising old notions about the city's history. A sampling of these includes Mary H. Blewett, *The Last Generation: Work and Life in the Textile Mills of Lowell, Massachusetts, 1910–1960* (Amherst: University of Massachusetts Press, 1990); Fred Coburn, *History of Lowell and Its People* (New York: Lewis Historical, 1920); John Coolidge, *Mill and Mansion: A Study of Architecture and Society in Lowell, Massachusetts, 1820–1865* (1942; 2d ed., Amherst: University of Massachusetts Press, 1993); Robert F. Dalzell, Jr., *Enterprising Elite: The Boston Associates and the World They Made* (New York: Norton, 1993); Thomas Dublin, *Women at Work: The Transformation of Work and Community in Lowell, Massachusetts, 1826–1860* (New York: Columbia University Press, 1981); Arthur L. Eno, Jr., ed., *Cotton Was King: A History of Lowell, Massachusetts* (Lowell: Lowell Historical Society, 1976); Hannah Josephson, *The Golden Threads: New England's Mill Girls and Magnates* (New York: Duell, Sloan, and Pearce, 1949); G. F. Kenngott, *The Record of a City: A Social Survey of Lowell, Massachusetts* (New York: Macmillan & Co., 1912); and Robert Weible, ed., *The Continuing Revolution: A History of Lowell, Massachusetts* (Lowell: Lowell Historical Society, 1991).

The history of the Boott Mills has been examined in depth by Laurence F. Gross in his book, *The Course of Industrial Decline: The Boott Cotton Mills of Lowell, Massachusetts, 1835–1955* (Baltimore: Johns Hopkins University Press, 1993) and in his essays, "Building on Success: Lowell Mill Construction and Its Results," in IA: *The Journal of the Society for Industrial Archeology.* 14, 2 (1988): 23-34 and "The Game Is Played Out: The Closing Decades of the Boott Mills," in Weible, *The Continuing Revolution*, 281-99. A thorough discussion of the architectural fabric of portions of the surviving Boott complex can be found in Laurence F. Gross and Russell A. Wright, *Historic Structure Report—History Portion: Building 6; The Counting House; The Adjacent Courtyard; and the Facades of Buildings 1 and 2. Boott Mill Complex, Lowell National Historical Park, Lowell Massachusetts* (Denver, Colorado: National Park Service, 1985).

Historical Archaeology in Context

Useful introductions to archaeology include Wendy Ashmore and Robert J. Sharer, *Discovering Our Past: A Brief Introduction to Archaeology* (Mountain View, Calif.: Mayfield Press, 1988); Brian M. Fagan, *Archaeology: A Brief Introduction* (5th ed., New York: HarperCollins, 1994). Introductory-level books on historical archaeology are appearing with increasing frequency, although to date no one book does justice to the field as a whole. Among those available, we recommend James Deetz, *In Small Things Forgotten: The Archaeology of Early American Life* (New York: Anchor Books, 1977); Ivor Noël Hume, *Historical Archaeology* (New York: Alfred A. Knopf, 1968) (though seriously outdated, much of its content remains relevant); and Charles E. Orser, Jr., and Brian M. Fagan, *Historical Archaeology: A Brief Introduction* (New York: HarperCollins, 1994). A thought-provoking collection of essays can be found in Bernard L. Herman and Lu An De Cunzo, eds., *Historical Archaeology and the Study of American Culture* (Winterthur, Del.: The Henry Francis du Pont Winterthur Museum, 1995). *Historical Archaeology*, published by the Society for Historical Archaeology, is the major journal for the field and, although focusing on North America, is global in scope; *Northeast Historical Archaeology*, the journal of the Council for Northeast Historical Archaeology, publishes articles pertaining to historical archaeology in the northeastern United States and eastern Canada. Only one comprehensive general work on industrial archaeology in North America is available: Robert B. Gordon and Patrick M. Malone, *The Texture of Industry: An Archaeological View of the Industries of North America* (New York: Oxford University Press, 1994). The Society for Industrial Archaeology publishes *IA: The Journal of the Society for Industrial Archaeology*.

Explorations of how historical archaeologists approach the analysis and use of documentary sources can be found in Mary C. Beaudry, ed., *Documentary Archaeology in the New World* (Cambridge: Cambridge University Press, 1988); Mary Ellin D'Agostino, Margot Winer, Elizabeth Prine, and Eleanor Casella, eds., *The Written and the Wrought: Complementary Sources in Historical Anthropology*, Kroeber Anthropological Society Papers, 78 (Berkeley, Calif.: Department of Anthropology, University of California at Berkeley, 1995); and Barbara J. Little, ed., *Text-Aided Archaeology* (Boca Raton, Fla.: CRC Press, 1992). Russell J. Barber has prepared a workbook on the use of sources in historical archaeology: *Doing Historical Archaeology: Exercises Using Documentary, Oral, and Material Evidence* (New York: Prentice-Hall, 1994). The standard reference for artifact identification in historical archaeology is Ivor Noël Hume's *Guide to Artifacts of Colonial America* (New York: Alfred A. Knopf, 1970), which, as the title indicates, focuses on the colonial period in North America. Students of nineteenth-century material culture lack such a comprehensive resource on artifact identification. A useful source to consult, however, is George L. Miller, Olive R. Jones, Lester A. Ross, and Teresita Majewski, comps., *Approaches to Material Culture Research for Historical*

Archaeologists: A Reader from Historical Archaeology (Tucson, Ariz.: Society for Historical Archaeology, 1991).

Overviews of the Lowell Archaeological Survey Project are provided in Stephen A. Mrozowski and Mary C. Beaudry, "The Archeology of Work and Home Life in Lowell, Massachusetts: An Interdisciplinary Study of the Boott Cotton Mills Corporation," IA: *The Journal of the Society for Industrial Archeology* 14, 2 (1988): 1-22 and in Stephen A. Mrozowski, "Historical Archaeology and the Industrial Revolution: The Lowell Archaeological Survey," *History News* 45, 4 (1990): 24-26. The results are reported in detail in a series of three monographs published by the National Park Service: Mary C. Beaudry and Stephen A. Mrozowski, eds., *Interdisciplinary Investigations of the Boott Mills, Lowell, Massachusetts*. vol. 1,: *Life in the Boarding Houses: A Preliminary Report*, Cultural Resources Management Series, 18 (Boston: National Park Service, North Atlantic Regional Office, 1987); *Interdisciplinary Investigations of the Boott Mills, Lowell, Massachusetts*, vol. 2,: The Kirk Street Agents' House, Cultural Resources Management Series, 19 (Boston: National Park Service, North Atlantic Regional Office, 1987); and *Interdisciplinary Investigations of the Boott Mills, Lowell, Massachusetts*, vol. 3,: *The Boarding House System as a Way of Life*, Cultural Resources Management Series, 21 (Boston: National Park Service, North Atlantic Regional Office, 1989).

Lowell's Urban Landscape

The built environment and urban landscape of Lowell are discussed in Thomas Bender, *Toward an Urban Vision: Ideas and Institutions in Nineteenth-Century America* (Baltimore: Johns Hopkins University Press, 1975); Randolph Langenbach, "From Building to Architecture: The Emergence of Victorian Lowell," *Harvard Architectural Review* 2 (1981): 90-105; Mary C. Beaudry, "The Lowell Boott Mills Complex and Its Housing: Material Expressions of Corporate Ideology," *Historical Archaeology* 23, 1 (1989): 19-32; Stephen A. Mrozowski and Mary C. Beaudry, "Archaeology and the Landscape of Corporate Ideology," in *Earth Patterns: Essays in Landscape Archaeology*, William M. Kelso and Rachel Most, eds., (Charlottesville: University Press of Virginia, 1990); Stephen A. Mrozowski, "Landscapes of Inequality," in *The Archaeology of Inequality*, ed. Randall McGuire and Robert Paynter, (Oxford: Basil Blackwell, 1991); William F. Fisher and Gerald K. Kelso, "The Use of Opal Phytolith Analysis in a Comprehensive Environmental Study: An Example from 19th-Century Lowell, Massachusetts," *Northeast Historical Archaeology* 16 (1987): 30-45; and Gerald K. Kelso, "Pollen-Record Formation Processes, Interdisciplinary Archaeology, and Land Use by Mill Workers and Managers: The Boott Mills Corporation, Lowell, Massachusetts, 1836-1942," *Historical Archaeology* 27, 1 (1993): 70-94 . For a series of essays on the archaeology of the urban environment, see A. R. Hall and H. K. Kenward, eds., *Environmental Archaeology in the Urban Context*, Council for British Archaeology

Research Reports 43 (London: Council for British Archaeology, 1982).

Living Conditions of Boott Mills Workers

Living conditions, hygiene, and sanitation in the Boott boardinghouses are discussed by Edward L. Bell, "A Preliminary Report on Health, Hygiene, and Sanitation at the Boott Mills Boarding Houses: An Historical and Archeological Perspective," in Beaudry and Mrozowski, eds., *Interdisciplinary Investigations of the Boott Mills*, vol. 1; Gerald K. Kelso, William F. Fisher, Stephen A. Mrozowski, and Karl J. Reinhard, "Contextual Archaeology at the Boott Mills Boardinghouse Backlots," in Beaudry and Mrozowski, editors, *Interdisciplinary Investigations of the Boott Mills*, vol. 3; Stephen A. Mrozowski, Edward L. Bell, Mary C. Beaudry, David B. Landon, and Gerald K. Kelso, "Living on the Boott: Health and Well Being in a Boardinghouse Population," World Archaeology 21, 2 (1989): 298-319; Mary C. Beaudry, "Public Aesthetics versus Personal Experience: Archaeology and the Interpretation of 19th-Century Worker Health and Well Being in Lowell, Massachusetts," *Historical Archaeology* 27, 2 (1993): 90-105; and David B. Landon, "Domestic Ideology and the Economics of Boardinghouse Keeping," in Beaudry and Mrozowski, *Interdisciplinary Investigations of the Boott Mills*, vol. 3.

Meal Times at the Boott

David H. Dutton analyzed the ceramics from the boardinghouse excavations in "Thrasher's China or Colored Porcelain: Ceramics from a Boott Mills Boardinghouse and Tenement," in Beaudry and Mrozowski, *Interdisciplinary Investigations of the Boott Mills*, vol. 3 and in "Thrasher's China or Colored Porcelain: Mealtime at the Boott" (M.A. thesis, Department of Archaeology, Boston University, 1990). Analysis of the documentary and zooarchaeological evidence is presented in David B. Landon, "Foodways in the Lowell Boardinghouses: The Historical and Zooarchaeological Evidence," in Beaudry and Mrozowski, *Interdisciplinary Investigations of the Boott Mills*, vol. 1; and in David B. Landon, "Faunal Remains from the Boott Mills Boardinghouses," in Beaudry and Mrozowski, *Interdisciplinary Investigations of the Boott Mills*, vol. 3.

Leisure Time at the Boott

Aspects of leisure behavior reflected by artifacts from the boardinghouses are discussed in Lauren J. Cook, "Tobacco-Related Material Culture and the Construction of Working Class Culture," and in Kathleen H. Bond, "'that we may purify our corporation by discharging the offenders': The Documentary Record of Social Control in the Boott Boardinghouses," and "The Medicine, Alcohol, and Soda

Vessels from the Boott Mills," all in Beaudry and Mrozowski, *Interdisciplinary Investigations of the Boott Mills*, vol. 3; and in Kathleen H. Bond, "Alcohol Use in the Boott Mills Boardinghouses: Tension between Workers and Management, a Documentary and Archaeological Study" (M.A. thesis, Department of Archaeology, Boston University, 1988).

Clothing and Personal Adornment

The artifacts of grooming and personal adornment from the boardinghouse back-lots were examined in detail by Grace H. Ziesing: "Analysis of Personal Effects from Excavations of the Boott Mills Boardinghouse Backlots in Lowell, Massachusetts," in Beaudry and Mrozowski, *Interdisciplinary Investigations of the Boott Mills*, vol. 3; as well as in her "Personal Effects from the Backlots of Boott Mills Corporate Housing in Lowell, Massachusetts: A Gender Study in Historical Archaeology" (M.A. thesis, Department of Archaeology, Boston University, 1990).

The Bigger Picture

For discussions of the decline of the textile industry in Lowell and its repercussions, see Gross, *Course of Industrial Decline* and essays in Weible, *Continuing Revolution*.

INDEX

Agents: diet of, 64–65; health of, 53, 57; house of, 39–42; responsibilities of, 5; yard of, 44

Alcohol consumption, 71–74

Animal remains, 31, 63–65

Appleton, Nathan, 1

Archaeobotanist, 29, 34

Archaeological subdisciplines: archaeobotany, 29; historical archaeology, xii–xiii, 11, 15, 18; industrial archaeology, 4, 15; palynology, 30; prehistoric archaeology, 15; zooarchaeology, 31, 34, 63

Architectural historians, 17

Artifacts: adornment, 75–80; botanical remains, 29, 47, 63–64; buttons, 79–80; ceramics, 24–26; clay pipes, 68–71; clothing, 55, 75–76; combs, 55, 78; definition of, 24–26; faunal remains, 32, 63–65; glass, 65, 73; metal, 77, 79; phytoliths, 30; pollen remains, 29–30, 63

Backyards, 7–9, 36–37, 43–48

Boott cotton mills: as example of corporate paternalism, 38–39, 66–67; history of, 1–3, 38–43; location of, 38

Building foundations, 11, 24

Ceramics: from agents' house, 64–65; from boardinghouse, 61–62; dating, 24–26

Clothing, 76

91

Computers, use of, in archaeological analysis, 34–36
Context: archaeological, 13; cultural, 13–14
Corporate paternalism at Boott mills, 2, 66
Croteau, Joseph, 7

Diet: of agents, 64–65; differences between workers, 24–25, 64; of unskilled workers, 62–64
Disease, 55–56
Documents, 18–21

Excavations, 16–18

Features: building foundations, 11, 23, 38; cellars, 23, 45; definition of, 11, 23–24; privies, 23, 45, 51–53, 56, 63; postholes, 23; wells, 23, 38, 53, 56
Flotation, 34
Foodways: definition of, 59; diet of agents, 64–65; diet of unskilled workers, 62–64; disposal of food and ceramics, 45; preparation of meals, 59–65; tableware of skilled workers, 25, 62; tableware of unskilled workers, 25, 61–62
Fox, Amanda, 5

Garbage, 45,
Graham, Blanche Pelletier, 7, 51–52, 63
Grid, 16

Health: in nineteenth century, 55–56; of unskilled workers, 52–53, 55–57
Hygiene: of agents, 57; in nineteenth-century, 55; of unskilled workers, 53–55

Immigrant workers, effectiveness of corporate paternalism on, 2–3
Industrial archaeology, 4, 15
Industrial revolution, 2
Interdisciplinary research, 35–36

Landscape, 38–39
Land use: by agents, 44; over time, 3, 7–9; by unskilled workers, 44–47
Larcom, Lucy, 39
Leisure time, 66–74; activities present in archaeological record, 67; of agents, 68; alcohol consumption, 71–74; beautification of backyard, 47–48; smoking, 67–71; of unskilled workers, 68, 73
Lowell: construction of, 38–39; history of, 1–3

Maggots, 45–47
Mill girls: effectiveness of corporate paternalism, 2–3, 66–67; implementation of corporate paternalism, 2–3, 66–67; replaced by immigrant workers, 2–3
Mill workers: immigrant workers and corporate paternalism, 66; mill girls, 2
Minimum vessel count, 35

Night cart system, 52

Oral history, 22–23

Palynologist, 30, 34
Parasites, 31–32
Phytoliths, 30, 34
Planned industrial communities and corporate paternalism at Boott cotton mills, 39
Plant remains, 28–30, 47

Pollen, 29–30
Probate, 19–21

Rats, 53

Salaries, 4
Sanitary conditions: and disease, 55–57; maggots, 45–47; parasites, 31–32; rats, 53; waste disposal systems, 52–53; water systems, 53, 55
Sirk, Saimon, 11
Skilled laborers, 4–7; material wealth of, 25, 62
Smoking, 67–71
Soil compounds, 32, 44
Stratigraphy, 26–28; cultural, 27–28; natural, 27

Tableware: of agents, 64; differences, 64; of skilled laborers, 25, 62; of unskilled laborers, 61–62
Tenements, 4, 7, 42
Textile economy, 3
Textile mills, 3

Unions, 3
Unskilled laborers: diet of, 62–64; health of, 55–57; leisure time of, 68, 73; material wealth of, 75–80

Vaccinations, 57

Wages, 4,80
Water system, 53, 55